Of Human Interaction

Of Human Interaction

Joseph Luft

San Francisco State College

 NATIONAL PRESS BOOKS

850 Hansen Way   Palo Alto, California 94304

Library of Congress Catalog Card Number: 76-84008

International Standard Book Numbers: 0-87484-134-8 (cloth)
0-87484-198-4 (paper)

Manufactured in the United States of America

9 8 7 6 5 4

To Rachel and Joshua

Contents

Introduction

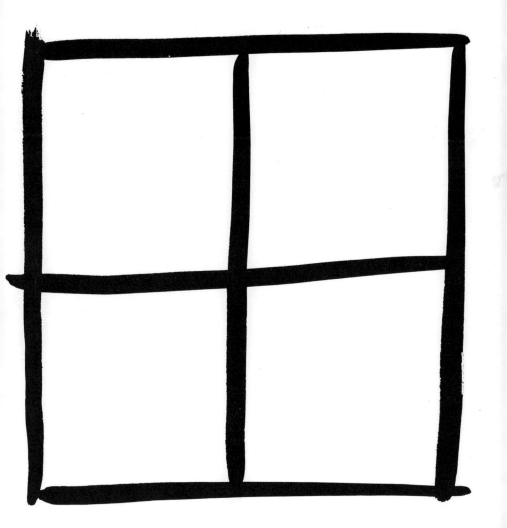

A Bias

There is ample precedent in the history of science for unevenness in the development of theory and application. Man could sail long before he understood the aerodynamics of hull and wing. Face-to-face interaction has always existed, but it will be a long time before we really understand how interaction works. The order is a large one: to understand man in relation to man. If our current knowledge is limited, spotty, contradictory, and foolish, that at least tells us where we are, and everyone is invited to improve on it.

What I attempt to do is set down ideas, impressions, and experiences about people interacting and try to make sense of it for myself. I have tried to remove the strictures of objectivity sufficiently to give me access to thoughts and hunches which ordinarily would sink for lack of methodological rigor. I was heartened to read along the way a comment in a recent book, *Small Group Research* by McGrath and Altman (1966, p. 86):

Given latitude and freedom, the scientist is an artist in that he will conduct research stemming from his own personal feelings, impressions, and insights. Of course, the scientist proceeds quite differently from the artist; he applies a specific set of procedures and criteria (the scientific method) to confirm or refute his hypotheses, intuitions, and hunches. But basically, the hunches are subjective in origin. This statement is not meant to be profound, but only to indicate that science is personal in some respects and that the scientist projects himself as a person into his work at certain points. And we value this personal aspect of science positively, for this is how creative concepts are forged and new directions charted.

Then, a bit later on, the authors state quite pointedly why they think the field is out of kilter (p. 87):

Thus, more and more focus has been placed on procedures, and less on substance. The dual nature of science seems at present to be greatly out of balance, elevating rigor of procedures to the detriment of creativity of substantive ideas. This lack of balance is both good and bad — good for the obvious reason that our armamentarium for dealing with ideas is steadily growing, but bad in the sense that it increases ideational sterility.

3   Introduction

McGrath and Altman come to these opinions after having scoured the field and prepared "a synthesis and critique" covering "approximately 250 small group research studies selected from a bibliography of over 2000 entries." Whatever the strengths and weaknesses of systematic investigation, there is of course no assurance that a more intuitive approach would yield greater returns. Nevertheless, there is a need for more ideas and hunches from all sources.

I believe that human interaction in a relatively free and unstructured setting soon will become a major preoccupation of behavioral scientists rather than a peripheral interest as it has been for several decades. I say this not because I am impressed by the present results of studies showing how much or how little people learn and change in this kind of setting. For an example of one such study, see Dunnette and Campbell (1969). Rather, what is impressive is that small groups offer an unparalleled opportunity to see human beings as they are. In a way, human interaction is not unlike a garden; from a distance, the scene looks colorful, idyllic. Up closer, you notice the variety of stones, earth, plants, and living organisms. Sit still in the garden for a long time so that you blend with the light and shadows and you begin to notice all kinds of action and behavior—lazy weeds nodding, ants trudging to work single file bearing impossible burdens, flowers courted by bright-winged insects, cheerful birds cannibalizing worms and bugs, mating calls, warning cries, things blooming and rotting, the exotic and the commonplace, disorder and frenzy alongside rhythm and pattern. Face-to-face groups reveal persons in their natural setting— with other people. They may serve as reference points to all other ways of studying human behavior in vivo. The beauty of it is that life goes on in these groups—life as it is. One may not have the talent to devise new theories of behavior, but at least one can not be charged with ignoring the subject.

Assumptions of the Johari Awareness Model

The Johari Window is a graphic model of interpersonal behavior that rests on a number of important assumptions. These assumptions are derived from selected theories of personality and social psychology. The assumptions reflect the biases of certain theorists and, of course, my own bias. Since the assumptions, or paradigms, are not shared by all or even most psychologists, there may be value in making them explicit. They are expressed here rather dogmatically, but only for the sake of brevity and clarity. See Coan (1968), Koch (1961), and Watson (1967) for further discussion.

1. Holistic vs. elementaristic units. Human behavior is best understood in terms of wholes or large units of behavior. Analyses of small units of behavior, such as what the muscles or sense organs are doing, are of value only as related to the total person and context.

2. Subjectivism vs. objectivism. The key to what is happening in a group or between persons is what is going on subjectively, what the feelings are. Subjective factors such as attitudes and values tell how the person sees himself and others and how he orders his world.

3. Irrationalism vs. rationalism. Though some of the events in groups and in persons can be viewed as being orderly and making good sense, behavior is influenced more by emotions and by largely irrational strivings; logic and reason play relatively minor roles in human interaction.

4. Behaving without awareness vs. behaving with awareness. The individual, like the group of which he is a part, has limited awareness of the sources of his own behavior and of the effects of his behavior on others. Crucial aspects of behavior are best understood by taking into account sources and determinants of behavior which are hidden from the person or about which he has limited understanding.

5. Quality vs. quantity. It is desirable to be able to measure and weigh the forces governing behavior. However, the best understanding comes with appreciation of qualitative differences of the processes of interaction between people and within groups. Qualities such as acceptance, collusion, influence, conflict, and trust, for example, are important even though they cannot be defined or measured with high precision.

6. Change states vs. structural properties. Attention should be directed to ongoing processes and the changes which are taking place. The search for an analysis of structural properties, though useful, is less important than an appreciation of change states.

7. Personal vs. nomothetic orientation. The experiencing individual or group deserves more stress than do abstract transpersonal rules. The problem is to discover general knowledge of persons and groups by direct concern with persons rather than by the application of abstractions which tend to lose humanness along the way.

8. Fluid vs. restrictive approaches. The first of these approaches favors "a basic predisposition to experience people and life in all their complexity in a rather relaxed fashion, while the latter suggests a tendency to deal with reality in a more controlling and compartmental fashion, through restriction of attention and through isolation of entities and events" (Coan, 1968).

Qualities of the Johari Awareness Model

The Johari Window,* as the concept is sometimes called, concerns awareness in human behavior. I have chosen to write "of human interaction" from the point of view of the awareness model because the model has a number of important qualities.

1. Awareness and consciousness are uniquely human attributes.

---

*It is fairly well known now that Johari does not refer to the southern end of the Malay Peninsula. That's Johore. Johari is pronounced as if it were Joe and Harry, which is where the term comes from. However, Harry Ingham of the University of California, Los Angeles, should not be held responsible for releasing this neologism. Dr. Ingham and I developed the model during a summer laboratory session in 1955, and the model was published in the *Proceedings of the Western Training Laboratory in Group Development* for that year by the UCLA Extension Office. The model also is described elsewhere (Luft, 1961 and 1963, for instance).

(Consciousness usually refers to what is felt within oneself and awareness, to that which is felt outside oneself. However, the terms are used interchangeably in these pages.) These states of knowing are supremely human and are of course central to any consideration of human interaction. The model starts with both states simultaneously.

2. Intrapersonal and interpersonal affairs are inextricably united. Regardless of one's perferred orientation in personality theory, identity and relationships are sufficiently intertwined so that it makes sense to consider them together. This can be done in the Johari framework without committing the theorist to a position which would violate the rest of his theory.

3. The model is essentially content free. No assumptions need be made about the sources of human behavior, such as growth, psychosexual or security needs, or other social and psychological needs and drives. Yet the model is sufficiently broad and open so that any of these assumptions could be applied. However, owing to the model's structure, the theorist can never lose sight of the various states of awareness and consciousness.

☐ *"In our culture, human beings tend to develop from a lack of awareness of the self as an infant to an awareness of and control over one's self as an adult. The adult who tends to experience adequate and successful control over his own behavior tends to develop a sense of integrity and feelings of self-worth."* — Chris Argyris (1961, p. 68)

4. The constructs implicit in each of the quadrants, lend themselves to verification. The open quadrant, Q1, the blind quadrant, Q2, and the hidden quadrant, Q3, are known to at least one person and thus are potentially confirmable. Even the unknown quadrant, Q4, which is known neither to the person nor to others, is *eventually* confirmable. (See page 63 for examples.)

5. The model can be applied to any human interaction. There is no inherent subject limitation. Gangs fighting, friends talking, executives leading, lovers loving—any of these interactions can be viewed and conceptualized within the model's framework. In this sense it is universally applicable.

6. The model is sufficiently uncomplicated so that it is readily used.

A wide range of people, from college freshmen to postdoctoral scholars, laymen as well as professionals, are able to grasp the model and use it to think about interaction without requiring extensive background in the behavioral disciplines.

7. The processes inherent in the model guide the reader to important characteristics of human interaction. For example, considerations of change in the first quadrant call attention to processes involved in moving to greater or lesser openness. Similarly, the processes involved in reducing or increasing blindness in the second quadrant focus on crucial developments in a relationship. The significance of any interpersonal event is sharpened when it is seen in the context of all four quadrants.

The scheme of the text is simply to apply the Johari awareness model to questions of human interaction. The questions are brought into focus with the aid of the four quadrants. Then the model is used to engage in speculation. For example, what happens in a group when someone gives an unsolicited interpretation of another's blind area? What happens to Q1, to Q3? The model helps to clarify changes in awareness and openness as well as changes in tension, defensiveness, and perhaps, hostility.

Certain universal questions are looked at through the model, questions about the effect of unknowns on human interaction, trust, levels of miscommunication, ancient and primitive leadership patterns, appropriate disclosure of self, and other related subjects.

The purpose of the text is twofold: to develop basic issues about human interaction with the aid of the model, and to illuminate interpersonal learning and the process of learning to learn. The meaning of observation and of feedback, for example, are considered to show how learning about behavior can be conceptualized, and some of the special qualities and problems in encounter groups (or T-groups, human relations laboratory groups, sensitivity groups, etc.) are discussed.

The two purposes overlap frequently since questions of learning and important issues such as trust and leadership are, of course, closely interrelated. The scheme of the text also lacks neatness and strict compartmentalization. Though the four quadrants of the Johari awareness model offer a rough sequence of attention, the model is applied now to one question and now to another. Such a scheme exhibits the rich potential of the model, however, and it suits the variety and inconsistency of human behavior.

I hope that this scheme is not too distracting to the reader. If he is already familiar with the four quadrants, he might enter the text at any point that interests him. He will not find a clear-cut beginning, middle, and end, but he will, I believe, discover portions of the text that stimulate his own observations, speculations, and discoveries about people interacting.

A Word about Experience-based Learning Groups

Since World War II but particularly in the last decade, interest in small group experience has expanded with the speed of an explosion. The reader may consult *T-Group Theory and Practice* by Bradford, Gibb, and Benne (1964) and the *Journal of Applied Behavioral Science* for the best background information on this development. Carl Rogers (1968) has made a particularly cogent observation of this phenomenon and its revolutionary implications for the future.

Many different terms are used to identify interaction groups, including T-groups ("T" for "training"), human relations training groups, laboratory groups, sensitivity training groups, personal growth groups, encounter groups, communication workshops, interpersonal groups, awareness groups, and learning groups. What goes on in the groups has been called group processes and group dynamics, among other things. The list goes on. However, it should be apparent that the names alone mean very little in the same sense that the names applied to teaching or counseling or management or psychotherapy mean very little by themselves.

In short, each group experience must be understood *on its own merits.* Even when two group leaders agree on basic theory, their groups may proceed with significant differences in direction, tempo, style, value, and results. Surely there are similarities, but no more so than similarities among different teachers or counselors or managers or psychotherapists.

Quadrant 1
Openness to the World

Brief Summary of the Johari Awareness Model

The four quadrants represent the total person in relation to other persons. The basis for division into quadrants is awareness of behavior, feelings, and motivation. Sometimes awareness is shared, sometimes not. An act, a feeling, or a motive is assigned to a particular quadrant based on who knows about it. As awareness changes, the quadrant to which the psychological state is assigned changes. The following definitions and principles are substantially the same as those in *Group Processes* (Luft, 1963, pp. 10-11). Each quadrant is defined:

1. Quadrant 1, the open quadrant, refers to behavior, feelings, and motivation known to self and to others.

2. Quadrant 2, the blind quadrant, refers to behavior, feelings, and motivation known to others but not to self.

3. Quadrant 3, the hidden quadrant, refers to behavior, feelings, and motivation known to self but not to others.

4. Quadrant 4, the unknown quadrant, refers to behavior, feelings, and motivation known neither to self nor to others.

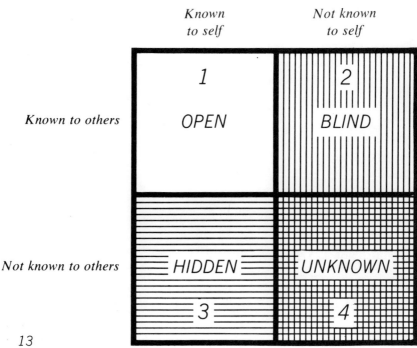

There are eleven principles of change:

1. A change in any one quadrant will affect all other quadrants.

2. It takes energy to hide, deny, or be blind to behavior which is involved in interaction.

3. Threat tends to decrease awareness; mutual trust tends to increase awareness.

4. Forced awareness (exposure) is undesirable and usually ineffective.

5. Interpersonal learning means a change has taken place so that quadrant 1 is larger, and one or more of the other quadrants has grown smaller.

6. Working with others is facilitated by a large enough area of free activity. It means more of the resources and skills of the persons involved can be applied to the task at hand.

7. The smaller the first quadrant, the poorer the communication.

8. There is universal curiosity about the unknown area, but this is held in check by custom, social training, and diverse fears.

9. Sensitivity means appreciating the covert aspects of behavior, in quadrants 2, 3, and 4, and respecting the desire of others to keep them so.

10. Learning about group processes, as they are being experienced, helps to increase awareness (enlarging quadrant 1) for the group as a whole as well as for individual members.

11. The value system of a group and its membership may be noted in the way *unknowns* in life of the group are confronted.

Quadrant 1, Openness to the World

The open quadrant, the area of free activity, is a window raised on the world — including the self. Behavior, feelings, and motivation known to self and known to others constitute the basis for interaction and exchange as these are commonly understood.

The simplest way to represent interaction is to use two figures, with arrows indicating the direction of the exchange. It is a bit more

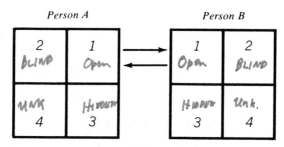

complicated to represent the exchange as occurring *within* the first quadrants: this shows the simultaneous effect of the exchange. How-

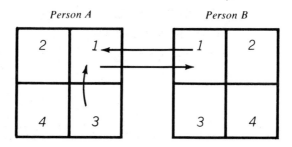

ever, the dynamics of the exchange are different for the two different individuals involved, as represented by the arrow from Q3 to Q1 of *A*. If *B* points to *A's* car and asks, "What happened to the fender?" the pointing and the spoken words as well as the tone and manner express a readily shared focus of exchange. *A*, however, can recall the parking accident that caused the dent; something known to him and not to *B* (in Q3) is then disclosed to Q1.

For each person, the open quadrant, Q1, varies in size within a definite range and around a modal area. For most occasions the modal area characterizes how open he is even though he may behave differently with different persons or with the same person at different times. Compare early and later states of friendship. Or note the large difference in a new group between early and later stages in the development of the group. In the figure shown, each horizontal bar between Q1 and Q3 represents a different degree of openness. Since Q3 is known to self and not to others, the individual has control of this area and may deliberately open or cover parts of his third quadrant.

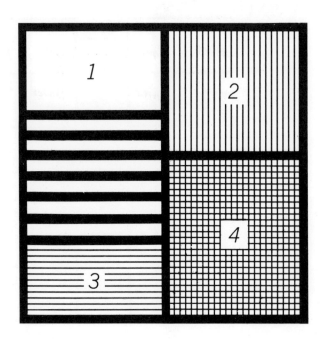

Though the awareness model itself is simple, any exchange can quickly complicate it. Therefore, it is important to apply the model in the simplest way so that the essentials of interaction are brought out. It is tempting to play in this manner with the interaction possibilities of each of the four quadrants, but before yielding it might be worthwhile to appreciate what this open or known quadrant means in man.

Adolf Portmann, a Swiss biologist, writing on "The Special Problem of Man in the Realm of the Living" (Portmann, 1965, p. 40) calls attention to this unique capacity:

The relative openness of an animal to the world is always circumscribed by a very narrow circle of possibilities, a circle that is never broken. By contrast, the openness of humans in experiencing the world cannot possibly be overestimated. We have only to remember that we are able to direct our attention at will to every detail, no matter how small, of the environment; that we are able at our pleasure to turn any single thing about us into an object of lifelong research. Anyone who has once become conscious of this freedom of concern, this open latitude for our direction of interest, will also understand something about the most basic factor of our human uniqueness. It is the same thing as that which philosophers have sometimes designated as "openness to the world." Each one of us is capable of standing, as it were, outside himself, of observing himself from an external vantage point, so to speak, and thus gaining detachment from himself and judging himself.

We do not have the slightest evidence that anything of this kind is possible for animals. The fact that men can direct their interests at will proves that their central nervous system is regulated with a view to this "openness." We know from our own experience, to be sure, that the degree of such openness can vary from man to man, that some men soon narrow their horizons and preclude themselves from wide areas of human possibility, while others preserve the greatest creative openness to a ripe old age. Yet notwithstanding such enormous individual differences, even the man with the most paltry human equipment is marked by the most potent of all special characteristics: openness to the world.*

Just looking anew at this extraordinary quality is itself challenging. It is so easy to take for granted. To be open to self, to others, to the world around us — by means of our senses and by our ability to transpose ourselves even outside ourselves — surely this identifies an essential quality of living as a human. It comes as a shock to realize that large individual differences in this ability exist, and that others are more open to experiencing the world than I. "Some men," as Portmann says, "soon narrow their horizons and preclude themselves from wide areas of human possibility, while others preserve the greatest creative openness to a ripe old age." I believe that one's usual openness, quadrant 1, can be changed. Knowledge, skill, awareness, and pleasure are determined by the magnitude of the first quadrant.

---

*From "The Special Problem of Man in the Realm of the Living" by Adolf Portmann in *Commentary,* November, 1965. Reprinted from *Commentary* by permission; Copyright © 1965 by the American Jewish Committee.

17   Quadrant 1, the Open Area

Thus to realize its existence, especially in relation to the other quadrants which are not open in one manner or another, is to establish an aspiration, if not a direction, for change.

One implication is that experience can be seen as an end in itself *and* as a means to an end. Certain experience is enlarging of this openness to the world and may be identified as true learning. Learning that closes us off is aptly described by Thorstein Veblen's phrase, "trained incapacity." The greatest single source for acquiring more openness is in the matrix of relationships to oneself and to others. Because each of us has, through experience, acquired some "trained incapacity" in functioning in this matrix, I believe that there is a genuine need to find interpersonal experiences which lead to more openness to the world. In the section on quadrant 3, I consider the relationship between self-disclosure and insight. Suffice to say at this point, indiscriminate or forced openness is neither useful nor desirable. Effective openness, however, takes work and some boldness because openness may be confused with nakedness.

In the Introduction to *Many Are Called* (Agee and Evans, 1966), a book of photographs of riders on the New York subways, James Agee writes (p. x):

They are members of every race and nation on earth. They are of all ages, all temperaments, of all classes, of almost every imaginable occupation. Each is incorporate in such an intense and various concentration of human beings as the world has never known before. Each, also, is an individual existence, as matchless as a thumbprint or a snowflake. Each wears garments which of themselves are exquisitely subtle uniforms, and badges of their being. Each carries in the posture of his body, in his hands, in his face, in the eyes, the signature of a time and place in the world upon a creature for whom the name immortal soul is one mild and vulgar metaphor.

The simplest or the strongest of these beings has been so designed upon by his experience that he has a wound and nakedness to conceal, and guards and disguises by which he conceals it. Scarcely ever, in the whole of his living, are these guards down. Before every other human being, in no matter what intimate trust, in no matter what apathy, something of the mask is there; before every mirror it is hard at work, saving the creature who cringes behind it from the sight which might destroy it.

Only in sleep (and not fully there), or only in certain waking moments of suspension, of quiet, of solitude, are these guards down; and these moments are rarely to be seen by the person himself, or by any other human being.*

Enlarging Quadrant 1

The idea that we all wear masks is as old as history itself. And it is equally well known that we are at times painfully transparent despite the effort to hide. These qualities, the need to cover up and the inevitability of inadvertent disclosure, immediately set the stage for the drama of human interaction. (See in this regard Goffman, 1955 and 1959.)

Artists, writers, people senstive and skillful in working with others, know about these conditions of human interaction. They are preoccupied by what they see and know and by what eludes them. The contrast between what a man hides and what he reveals without awareness stirs curiosity in all of us. And this is just what is captured in the photographs by Walker Evans in *Many Are Called* (Agee and Evans, 1966). In effect he has seen and photographed the faces of all of us, and James Agee describes how rigidly and permanently we are locked in from ourselves, from others, from openness to the world.

Charlotte Selver is not quite as pessimistic as Agee. She is interested in "Sensory Awareness and Total Functioning" (Selver, 1957). She quotes from Ernest Schachtel (1947): "The average adult . . . has ceased to wonder, to discover. . . . It is this adult who answers the child's questions and, in answering, fails to answer them, but instead acquaints the child with the conventional patterns of his civilization, which effectively close up the asking mouth and shut the wondering eye." Schachtel continues, "Even if, in modern civiliation, the capacity

---

*From *Many Are Called* by James Agee and Walker Evans, published by Houghton Mifflin. Reprinted by permission.

for such fresh experience has largely been deadened, most people, unless they have become complete automatons, have had glimpses of the exhilarating quality that makes fresh experience, unlabeled, so unique, concrete and filled with life." Charlotte Selver goes on to talk about her own work. She sees people, a cross section of the adult population, who come to her for help; they appear to have lost touch with themselves, their bodies, their feelings. They characteristically ask for direction, instruction, and guidance because they have learned too well the lessons in growing up: do not trust yourself, others know best, tune in to the important people around you, ignore your own promptings (Selver, 1957):

> People who come to the studio to have me tell them what to do to get a good posture — how to move, how to stand, how to sit — or in order to be exercised, are quite astonished at first, when they are invited to become more restful, to give up the "doing" so that they can listen better to what their body has to tell them. We need quiet for self-experience — quiet and awakeness. We need permissiveness too, permissiveness to all the subtle changes which may be needed.
>
> It is easier at first for people to lie down on the floor, permitting time to perceive, or, as we say, to "sense" themselves. We ask, "What can one feel of one's own organism, what of happenings within — not what one *knows* of one's body, or what one *thinks* about it, or believes *somebody else expects one to feel of it,* but what one *actually senses,* no matter what comes to the fore?" Sensations come gradually; one can not force them. The more one expects the less will come. We learn gradually not to expect anything at all, but to register what is happening in our organism. This physical self-experience is for many people entirely new, often stirringly so.*

Selver's work could be illustrated in Johari terms. Internal behavior tensions, needs from within, are attended to, so that they become recognizable in Q1. Various exercises and activities, such as deliberate breathing, feeling one's weight on the floor, moving one's limbs, are done in a way that helps the person to receive ongoing sensations from

---

*From "Sensory Awareness and Total Functioning" by Charlotte Selver in *General Semantics Bulletin,* numbers 21 and 22, published by the Institute of General Semantics. Reprinted by permission.

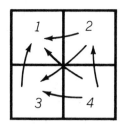

his own body. These inner impressions are always there but become walled off and lost. Eventually, by restoring contact with self through exploration and sensing, one rediscovers more of one's selfness. In this way, one may restore part of the lost openness to the world, the world of inner life.

Repeatedly, people report how good it feels to be in touch with oneself. For Selver, this experience is valuable because she believes that all tensions and anxieties, indeed all feelings, are physically and psychologically present simultaneously. Awareness of and sensitivity to inner states is therefore fundamental to being a person instead of a robot. I refer to Charlotte Selver's work because it so clearly expresses a key aspect of the intrapersonal equation without which interpersonal perception and behavior make little sense.

One of the figures here shows constriction and a greatly reduced open quadrant. Behavior and feelings for the individual represented would be limited in range, variety, and scope. Stereotypy and inflexibility would characterize this person's relationships. Generally, interaction would tend to be conventional and limited, and the person's upbringing would be psychologically deprived and unfree. However, the interaction model assumes that all humans are responsive to

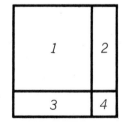

Psychological constriction and openness,
hypothetical extremes

present groups and individual relationships, and that change or learning could follow if opportunities for new interaction occur. The degree of rigidity is a function both of the size of Q1 and of the boundaries between quadrants.

The other figure represents an individual whose interactions are characterized by great openness to the world. Much of his potential has been developed and realized. The simple square design distorts this fellow because it is obvious that, if anything, the area of the unknown for him may be even larger than it is for the average person, and that his blind and hidden quadrants might be very complex. Since he has a high degree of awareness of self, he is less preoccupied with defensiveness and distortion. He has more access to inner resources. He is not overly involved in self-scrutiny or soul-searching. As described earlier (Portmann, 1965, p. 40), openness to the world implies a developed and ever-growing state, an experiencing, doing, enjoying, struggling, changing, creating, dreaming, agonizing, renewing, problem-solving, appreciating state of being with self and with others. Large tolerance for anxiety in self (especially in doing original things and in confronting many kinds of unknowns) and for the acceptance of differences in others are qualities in persons with a large first quadrant. Boundaries between quadrants are flexible and permeable. The flow of feelings and of ideas suggests a high capacity for all kinds of experience, conflict, enjoyment, and personal productivity.

Interaction between Two Persons Who Vary in Degree of Openness

Since, by definition, Q1 is what is known to self and known to the other person, it follows that, at any given moment, the size of Q1 is identical for each person in interaction.

But what if one person had greater openness in general? Some knowledge and awareness moves from the first into the third (hidden) quadrant simply because the other person lacks the capacity to know it. When an adult interacts with a young child the adult ordinarily assumes that there are many things of which he is aware and the child is not. The adult's third quadrant increases in size and, depending on the child, the adult's open quadrant is limited to the range of the child's awareness. Of course, the child is aware of things not available to the adult, and these reside in the child's third quadrant.

The figures here represent two persons whose open quadrants are typically of unequal size. Person B can more readily reduce his first

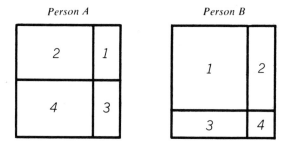

quadrant to A's size than vice versa. Thus, Q1, the area of behavior, feelings, and motivation known to both, becomes the same size for each.

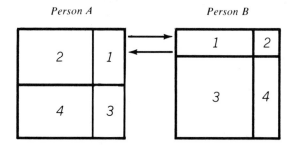

The area for Q1 is the same for both, but the shape is different because each person varies with regard to what is not known to him as well as to what he keeps hidden. In the case of A and B, quadrants 2, 3, and 4 are unequal.

During interaction, each person perceives something in the other of which the other is unaware. The amount of behavior, feeling, and motivation perceived depends most heavily on the size of the open quadrant, Q1. But other factors are also involved.

Actually, all four quadrants, which make up the total personality, affect what one perceives in another. We tend to see in others the things with which we are preoccupied, whether we are aware of them or not. The Machiavellian individual tends to view others in terms of manipulation or control. The affect-hungry person is more apt to see potential for feelings of warmth and closeness. The suspicious one may be more attuned to real or imagined threats in another. I use these oversimplified types only to illustrate a point, since obviously people are more complex than unidimensional traits.

There is a relationship between Q1 and Q2 because what is known to self and known to others offers clues for understanding the other person's blind spot. For example, if I knew you received bad news from home, I might be able to make more sense out of my observation that today you were not hearing others as well as you usually do.

Quadrant 2
the Blind Area

Quadrant 2, the Blind Area

The curious idea that man is unable to see and understand a good part of himself despite his intelligence and self-consciousness has been voiced by William James and by poets and philosophers centuries before Freud. The graphic analogy for Freud was the iceberg; man's mind was mostly submerged, only a small part appearing above the waterline.

Quadrant 2 shows roughly the same picture with the added detail that some of man's behavior and his motives are known to others and not to himself.

There is still a very large quadrant 4 about which no one is informed, neither the man himself nor the people who know him.

☐ *"Individuality is found in feeling; and the recesses of feeling, the darker blinder strata of character [emphasis added] are the only places in the world in which we catch real fact in the making, and directly perceive how events happen, and how work is actually done. Compared with this world of living individualized feelings, the world of generalized objects which the intellect contemplates is without solidity or life."* — William James (1902, p. 379)

Having blind spots about my own behavior means that I am eternally vulnerable to others. Knowing I am blind or partially blind helps a great deal, but does not resolve the dilemma. Knowing others have blind areas helps a bit more, but still does not remove the predicament.

At any rate, how do I deal with the embarrassing prospect? The answer of course is to get on with the major curriculum, to learn to "know thyself." How do I begin? The subject, me, is so simple, yet complicated, where do I start? Can I learn about the things I don't know about myself that others seem to see so clearly, without hurting them or myself? I know a few things about others of which they are unaware — will I have to spill all in order to get them to level with me? Won't this change my relationship with them? Why are people so hypocritical; if they know something why don't they speak out? The truth won't hurt, or will it? Perhaps it would be better all around to simply ignore the blind areas and to agree to deal only with what is in the open for all parties concerned. I see no point in embarrassing people by letting them know I know something about them of which they are unaware. After all, we are not barbarians. A man should live and let live by learning how to behave diplomatically. Tact will do the job. Learn to be discrete and tactful and this whole unpleasant half-blind affair can be dropped.

Unfortunately, it cannot be dropped. Blind areas increase the hazards of living with ourselves and with others even if it may add a note of unselfconscious charm.

People who know you well know a great deal about you of which you may be unaware. Even on short contact, another person may discern qualities in you that you are not ready or able to see.

A bright and experienced technical man quickly achieved recognition in a new encounter group as an effective member. However, a few people revealed some time later that though they were impressed by his intelligence and articulateness they were antagonized by him. At first they could not say what made them distrust him. Eventually they could feel his dislike for some of the group members who were not as bright or as well trained as he was. He made them feel inferior and less worthwhile as human beings. At first he denied having such arrogant attitudes but a number of people pointed out how he behaved. They said that he ignored comments of less capable members, occasionally interrupted them, poked fun at their difficulties and at times was patronizingly courteous. Some of these traits he half-perceived in himself. For example, what they saw as arrogance he had seen as self-assertiveness; what they saw as using jokes to belittle others he thought was a fine sense of humor in himself. Nor could he understand why his courteous manners were seen as patronizing until they pointed out the manipulative way he used courtesy. Thus, he half-perceived himself correctly. His behavior and his motives in the first and second quadrants were more clearly revealed to him in terms of the effect he had on other people. He was not very happy to learn these things about himself, but he came to realize they were accurate perceptions of his behavior which must have affected not only the strangers in the group but his colleagues at work, as well as his family and friends back home. He spent considerable time trying to learn more about his effect on others as well as reflecting about the meaning of this for himself.

How does one learn more about one's blind area, Q2? There are many answers, but nobody really knows. This is not sophistry but an accurate statement of prevailing knowledge. And for very good reason—the most complicated subject is man, man in relations with others and in relation to himself. Nothing is more important; and yet systematic, confirmable inquiry has only just begun in this century.

But surely learning about himself and his blind area has been going on since the beginning of time; man must have learned a great deal. Yes, he has, but how much is valid is still unknown. Powerful suggestions come from all quarters:

1. You learn best by experience.
2. Experience is the worst teacher as well as the best.
3. Art is the great teacher.
4. "Art is but a mild narcotic; a temporary refuge" (Freud, 1929, p. 34).
5. History informs man of his true nature.
6. Literature reveals the truth.
7. Life is a mystery and religion offers the only meaning.
8. Life is absurd and there is no meaning, hidden or revealed.
9. Science alone discovers what the world and man are all about.
10. Science is limited to the simplest regularities.
11. Psychotherapy is the best way to learn about oneself.
12. Psychotherapy has failed to obtain verifiable results.
13. A good education is the best we can do.
14. Education is adapted for the past, certainly not for the present.

These trackings of our will to learn do not by any means exhaust the catalog of efforts to overcome our psychological blindness. In effect, we are compelled to take our stand behind two positions. The first is to continue the struggle for enlightenment using the best of the known ways, and adding to these with whatever ingenuity and originality we can bring to bear. The second is to recognize that we will remain blind and unaware, to some extent, regardless of our growth and actualization, and to develop a degree of humility in the face of this reality. A pessimistic view? I don't think so, unless one is determined that the tragic and the comic both can be expunged from interpersonal experience.

The Matrix of Interaction between Two Persons

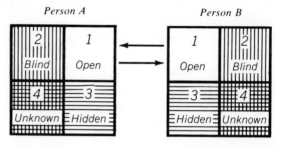

Person *A* perceives the first and second quadrants of *B*. *A* is aware of his own Q3, and though *B* knows of the existence of *A*'s Q3 he is not aware of the feelings and thoughts there unless *A* discloses them.

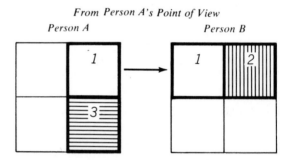

From Person A's Point of View

B perceives Q1 and Q2 of *A* and his own Q3. *A* and *B* share awareness of whatever is mutually held in their first quadrants: behavior in the open. This does not necessarily mean that *A* and *B* are in agreement

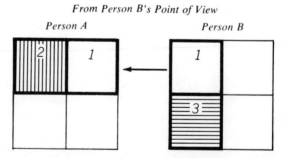

From Person B's Point of View

about what they both know. *A* interacts with *B* as *A* sees *B* (Q1 and Q2 of *B*). However, *A*'s perception of *B* consists of two parts, the subjective and the objective. The subjective is the purely personal, i.e., what A alone perceives. The objective part, in human interaction, is what is consensually shared with others. However, for A there is *no division into the objective and the subjective;* it is all of a piece. In other words, some of A's perception of B has consensual reliability (objectivity) and some of A's perception of B lacks this reliability (has little or no concurrence with others).

It should be clear that we are discussing consensual reliability and not validity. Obviously, consensus and validity are not necessarily the same thing. When criteria of validity exist, we could rely on these and set aside consensus. For example, production records are better than appearance for judging a worker's competence. However, interpersonal relations are based primarily on the perceived qualities in behavior and not on more valid elements. When A looks at B and interacts with B, A is influenced by his own *four* quadrants. *What* A *sees in* B *tells at least as much about* A *as about* B. What A, C, D, E, F, G, H, I J, and K see in B in common has reliability, of course, and it also has a higher probability of being "true" or valid than what A sees alone, assuming that some criterion of validity may be brought to bear. This probability is increased if the collection of persons $A...K$ includes generally diverse points of view. In a group workshop, as in any group, participants study each other long enough to determine whether the members are sufficiently free to have relatively independent perceptions.

We tend to pigeonhole each other very quickly and then to search for confirmation of our own stereotyping. Part of the delight in small group exploration is the way we come to modify our impressions of each other. Rarely do we know what moves another to change his impression of us.

In a heterogeneous group, one member was conspicuously erratic, being at times self-confident and assertive, and at other times weak and self-critical. He had a way of annoying the group and it was hard to tell whether he did this out of weakness or strength. The group exhausted its patience and eventually shunted him aside. They became interested in many other things which seemed more important and more interesting. A few days later several quieter members were able to make progress on their own after a long period of holding back. A few unobtrusive things the leader did when the erratic member was disciplined by the group made a great difference to these less secure members. The leader had not lost interest in the erratic member, whether he acted out of weakness or of strength; there had been some minor conversation between them to which no one seemed to pay much attention. However, the shy members recalled this episode vividly for it crystallized the way they perceived the leader as a person genuinely interested in and concerned with all of the participants.

The Hidden Area and the Blind Spots

One of the remarkable things about your hidden area, Q3, is that it is an important key to your own blind area, Q2. Here is a schematic view of what happens in Q1, Q2, and Q3 for a typical person-in-relationship:

	Known to self	Not known to self
Known to others	1	2
Not known to others	3	4

Behavior or feelings hidden from others is disclosed, and quadrant 1, the open area, is enlarged.

The other person now sees more of you in the open and also sees more of your blind area. You come through less distorted. He in turn can react more specifically and appropriately to you, thereby becoming

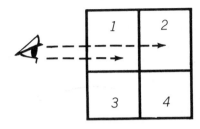

a bit more clear in relation to you. There is also a tendency for the other person to reciprocate by being more open toward you. With both now sharing greater open areas, Q1, there is more basis for trust and less defensiveness.

With less distortion, with less need to protect self, you are more apt to recognize behavior to which you were previously blind, as the other person brings out or reacts to behavior and feelings in your second quadrant. Robert Frost has described some important aspects of the process (Frost, 1949, p. 27):

Revelation

We make ourselves a place apart
    Behind light words that tease and flout,
But oh, the agitated heart
    Till someone really finds us out.

'Tis pity if the case require
    (Or so we say) that in the end
We speak the literal to inspire
    The understanding of a friend.

But so with all, from babes that play
    At hide-and-seek to God afar,
So all who hide too well away
    Must speak and tell us where they are.*

Our perceptions and understanding of each other are always less than perfect. Usually we have spotty and limited views of each other. No wonder then that we feel justified in resisting being told about our own behavior since the other is ignorant of so much we do know about ourselves, represented by the size of our third quadrants. There are of course other important psychological reasons for not accepting what others tell us about our blind spots. Man may be provoked, delighted, bruised, nurtured, and sustained by others, but he grows from within.

Interacting Alone

We carry each other around in our heads and continue interaction even after the other person is not present. An important aspect of human interaction is this interaction before or after being in the physical presence of the other. Anticipatory interaction with the other in our minds serves to prepare us for the exchange, and in certain important occasions may be crucial. In our heads we play both roles, making due allowance for the known and unknown quadrants of ourselves and the other individual, as we understand them.

Usually, the imaginary interactions are casually done, and it is rewarding to catch oneself playing these scenes. They tell important things about ourselves and about the particular relationship. Frequently, this foreplay occurs as a function of anxiety in the relationship, and more specifically where there is some danger. Then we plan the interaction with greater deliberation. "If he says this, I'll say that," ruminates the employee going in to see the boss, "and if he does so-and-so, I'll do thus-and-so."

More interaction-in-the-head occurs, however, *after* real interaction than before. This is a guess on my part, but I believe it can be shown empirically. Most interactions are sufficiently open-ended so that the unexpected might occur. This is especially so in view of the presence of the four quadrants in each participant.

After the interaction in vivo, we can go over the events in order to savor the experience or to appreciate more clearly what was going on, what went wrong and what went right. Important work in the service of self may take place, awareness may deepen, and problems may be centered on the mind's examining table for a more careful inspection.

In the course of any interaction our blind areas show themselves to others in characteristic ways. We distort or forget or exaggerate things; we overreact or underreact. We say gauche things or we don't hear things. We imagine something is intentional when it is not and we laugh in the wrong places. Others talk funny (strange), or so it appears to us when our blind areas are involved. We become silent or we express ourselves in a way which others note but we are oblivious to. Thus, it is no wonder that after the interaction we go home and try to make sense of some of these peculiar little occurrences. It may be a bit painful to see retrospectively what others were seeing all along. But we may also learn by going over the ground a second or third time.

The enjoyment of human interaction also occurs, in part, after the real interaction is over. We can feel the richness or the warmth of an exchange again and again. Sometimes, the humor is evident only retrospectively, a bonus we can enjoy by ourselves or recapitulate and share with others.

Forced Exposure — Psychological Rape

As mentioned, the blind area contains behavior, feelings, and motivation not accessible to the person, but which others can see. They therefore have the option of forcibly revealing what the individual is not ready to perceive. Examples of feelings and needs difficult to face:

1. Feelings of inadequacy, incompetence, and impotence.
2. Sensitivity to rejection or affection.
3. Need to punish or to be punished.
4. Guilt-laden and depressive moods.
5. Passive-dependent feelings, especially in men and in women who have high achievement aspirations.
6. Intense feelings of loneliness and isolation.
7. Conflictful feelings for loved ones.
8. Powerful needs to control or to manipulate others.
9. Qualities in the person that he cannot tolerate in others.
10. Feelings of unworthiness and despair.

This list is only illustrative and is not meant to be exhaustive. However, the items are sufficiently common to have some relevance to any group of people.

Forcing Q2 behavior into Q1, out into the open, can be traumatic. Perhaps the essential idea behind psychological trauma is disclosure so violent that the normal integrative processes do not work. The normal forgetting process fails, or the process by which a thought or feeling recedes back into Q2 or Q4 breaks down.

High anxiety and turmoil may result. Fortunately, a number of safety devices exist within the individual and within the group so that protection against psychological rape is possible. In the individual denial of the forced disclosure is probably the most common reaction. There are other ways of avoiding, ignoring, rationalizing, or otherwise deflecting the disclosure. Sometime later the individual may, after considerable experience and growth, look back and recognize the earlier attack-and-denial as the first intimation of new awareness. More often, defenses around the troubled feelings become tighter and the emotional issue buried still deeper; another reason for sensitivity and skill in conducting such groups.

☐ *"The things that are near and dear to you are very difficult to see."* – Dorothea Lange, artist-photographer, in a televised interview

The protective resources in the group are considerable. Members witnessing forced disclosure may come to the aid of the victim. Obser vations of behavior in Q2 as alleged may be challenged by others. If the observations happen to be accurate they may turn on the attacker, challenging *his* motives. They may raise questions about his lack of sensibility or his poor judgment. The group may work to improve the level of trust by opening basic *group* issues. The attacking incident itself is examined in the perspective of ongoing group processes. For example, if *A* attacked *B* by forcibly disclosing some element in *B*'s blind quadrant, the group may concern itself with the fact that *A* and *B* have been vying for leadership if this is a significant group issue not previously discussed.

In one group, a sudden effort by a member to reveal something in the blind area of a weaker member was examined by the group and found to be related to the approaching time for ending the series of group meetings. Apparently the unwarranted disclosure was an effort to prolong the meetings. There was recognition of a general reluctance to leave. Bringing this into the open not only protected the weaker member but gave the group another opportunity to work on feelings about terminating meaningful human relationships.

There are ways of helping people to come to terms with blindness in groups and unawareness in interpersonal relations without destroying either the group or the relationship. The sections dealing with appropriate disclosure (page 127), interpersonal confirmation (page 135), trust (page 136), and games without end (page 83) are particularly relevant. These discussions are aimed at the identification of basic principles underlying human interaction and are not intended as a "how-to-do-it" guidebook. Interaction problems are selected to emphasize the functions of awareness and unawareness between persons and within groups.

Q2 and Oedipus Rex

A dramatic illustration of interaction dealing with the second quadrant (blind area) is found in an early scene of *Oedipus Rex*. Thebes, the city state, is plagued by disasters and death, indicating the gods are displeased. Citizens appeal to King Oedipus who determines to find out what is wrong. He sends his brother-in-law Creon to the Oracle at Delphi. The message Creon brings back warns that the evil doer, the murderer of the prior ruler, King Laius, is in their midst. Oedipus, angry and suspicious, interrogates everyone who had any knowledge of the death of King Laius. Teiresias, a blind prophet who had warned Laius that he would die at the hands of his own son, is now an old man. He is brought before Oedipus who insists that Teiresias reveal everything he knows about the murder and about his prophecy and warning to King Laius. Teiresias is aware of Oedipus' role in the tragedy but refuses to talk:

> *Oedipus:* What! You do know something and will not tell us?
> *Teiresias:* I do not intend to torture myself, or you. Why persist in asking? You will not persuade me.
> *Oedipus:* What a wicked old man you are! You'd try a stone's patience! Out with it! Have you no feelings at all?
> *Teiresias:* You call me unfeeling. If you could only see the nature of your own feelings . . .*

The exchange between King Oedipus and the blind prophet Teiresias is a dramatic illustration of the hidden (Q3) and blind (Q2) quadrants. The interplay between feelings and awareness is evident in every line. The power to change rests on the shifts in awareness from covered to open quadrants. As a seer, Teiresias has the extraordinary ability to see what Oedipus cannot see in himself and thus holds power over him. Another unusual aspect of this interaction is that the one who is blind to his own behavior is forcing the other, who is physically blind but psychologically perceptive, to disclose what that behavior is. Few

---

*From *Oedipus Rex* by Sophocles, translated by Dudley Fitts and Robert Fitzgerald, published by Harcourt, Brace & World. Copyright 1936, 1960 by Harcourt, Brace & World. Reprinted by permission.

are that brave or foolhardy. Teiresias is insulted by Oedipus and in rage smashes back at the king by disclosing his unpardonable crimes.

The Oedipus story is a dramatic study of the four quadrants. The misery in the land moves to a crisis, and though the evidence of plague and disturbance is known to all in Q1, no one can understand what caused the unrest. This is a Q4 condition which initially is known to the gods but not to the king nor to the citizens.

Little by little the unknown is made known. The Oracle at Delphi brings out some information. The prophet Teiresias adds more, drawing on his own special knowledge in his hidden area, Q3. The shepherd also contributes from his memory (Q3) the fact that he did remove the baby from King Laius but that the child was not destroyed. Then Queen Jocasta adds more from her third quadrant and even Oedipus himself contributes from recollections of his early background. Perhaps the sin of pride, or hubris, in Oedipus is based at least in part on the force and arrogance with which he pries out knowledge and behavior in all those around him. His certainty of his own innocence, his belief that what he was doing was absolutely right, drives him on even though the prophet and the queen and others warn him to desist and not to tamper too much with fate and the unknown. But Oedipus takes no heed; he presses on even as fear begins to grip him.

Although Oedipus is responsible for exposing his acts of patricide and incest, he is not aware of these deeds themselves. That is, he is actually innocent of the fact that the man he killed was his father and that the woman he married was his mother. Simon Lesser in his book *Fiction and the Unconscious* (1960) interprets the dramatic theme in a way that takes account of Oedipus' innocence. Lesser believes that the play is universally successful because the feelings that might move one to patricide or to incest exist in the unconscious of all men, in the classical Freudian sense. These feelings are activated when one sees the play, and they re-arouse anxiety and dread in all of us. Finally, when Oedipus is destroyed as a king and blinded as a man, the audience accepts this tragic denouement even though he is technically innocent. The witness is relieved of his own anxiety and accepts the psychological law which holds that such feelings must be subdued at all cost.

Perceiving and Knowing

Oedipus blinds himself because he saw too much. The idiom is a familiar one: to see is to perceive and to perceive is to know. To know means more likelihood of becoming aware and hence of changing. Now you must live with yourself in the new awareness. In the Johari principles of change the notion of universal ambivalence toward exploring the unknown in self and in others is expressed. Every change appears to contain some risk. Whatever difficulties we now face, we are at least acquainted with them. Up to a point, exploring the unknown is exciting and vitalizing. We seem to have built-in sensors to alert us or warn us when we go too far.

Maslow makes an important distinction in *The Psychology of Science* (1966) between the safe, defensive, conservative seekers and the growth-oriented, risk-taking seekers. The former explore within safe, known bounds, and the latter search in new areas. The original artist represents this exploration best, although it may be recognized as well in scientists and, of course, in nonintellectual fields.

In interpersonal relations we can observe the same phenomenon. Some individuals are more apt to interact in a way that induces fresh exploration of self and others. Perhaps most of us tend to stay within safer areas of exchange, sacrificing excitement for stability.

☐ *"We may be entering the era of the second quadrant and, if so, then we are in for a true revolution in human affairs. It will be a time when all men recognize, acknowledge, and concede that they lack awareness of some areas of their own behavior, behavior which others can clearly see and apprehend."* — J. L.

Professionals in the mental health field are sometimes accused of developing interaction techniques which are aimed at the excitement of exploring the unknowns in others while retaining the benefits of safety and cover for themselves. The humanistic and existential practitioners are particularly critical of this stance. As I understand their criticism, interpersonal interaction is seen as therapeutically meaningful when the readiness to face change is shared by *all* involved. Appropriate disclosure of self (see page 127) is, of course, consistent with this point of view. Overdisclosing of self would then appear as inappropriate as not disclosing enough.

Oedipus uncovered his crimes and his sins publicly. There was no chance to hide his guilt even if he were so inclined.

How to Annoy Your Friends Clinically

It's rather simple to annoy your friends and relatives. Just tell them something about themselves of which they are not aware. Whether it is true or not is only slightly relevant. Questionable validity will rarely dissuade the psychopest, one who gives his unsolicited interpretation or judgment of a person's behavior or motives.

The psychopest purports to be a specialist in the second quadrant of the Johari Window. Occasionally, he trespasses into the third quadrant, where by definition he lacks awareness. His advantage stems from the fact that each of us lacks awareness (Q2 or Q4) about ourselves in some aspects of our being.

The psychopest may inform you that you are trying to manipulate others or that you are being defensive or self-deceiving or that you are acting out of guilt-laden or fearful motives. He has an endless array of tidbits like these to choose from. And his motives are of the best; he merely wants to help you, whether you've asked for his help or not.

It is in the nature of charges about your Q2 area that you cannot deal easily with them. How can you deny that you are trying to influence others or that you are self-deceiving? However, you have several alternatives open to you:

1. You can ignore the psychopest (but you have to be pretty breezy to brush him aside).

2. You can ask for the psychopest's motives and credentials. It is far more comfortable and interesting to examine him.

3. You can check with others who have witnessed the same events.

4. You can request that he act like a psychopest.

If he carries out your request you might compliment him. If you are in a group, you might invite others to keep tabs on the psychopest to see that his efforts are rewarded. He is now in a paradox. In order to attack you he must carry out your directive, thereby confirming your prediction of his behavior (see, for further discussion of this technique, Jackson, 1962).

This fourth alternative may look like fighting fire with fire, but its main purpose is to help the psychopest gain awareness and control of this aspect of his behavior. Obviously it will not work with persons who have an inordinate need to be one up on others all the time. Fencing and fighting come in infinite variety and, of course, constitute an important mode of human interaction. But the sting may be removed temporarily and a group may be able to continue its work while the psychopest struggles with his own learning.

Quadrant 3
The Hidden Area

Quadrant 3, the Hidden Area

What is known to self and not known to others is the private realm. Here discretion reigns. The third quadrant is a repository for what you know, including what you know about yourself and about others, and prefer to keep to yourself. It may include what is simply not relevant to a particular relationship, for example, your appendicitis scar, the mortgage on your house, your son's bed-wetting, your aversion to people who smile too much, your discomfort with bossy women, your secret enjoyment of deferential colleagues, or your self-criticism for having been brusque with a clerk for a typing error.

At any moment you can reveal one of these private facts or reactions, make it part of quadrant 1, and have it take its place in the ongoing relationship. You may suspect that such disclosure will stimulate a similar or related disclosure by the other party with whom you are interacting.

In the early phases of a relationship with a new acquaintance or with an associate on the job, the Q3-to-Q1 action may be most frequent. Strangers in a new group tend to open the small first quadrant by voluntary shifts of private knowledge into the open. Involuntary disclosures are of course also being made. Social custom actually prescribes the kinds of things ordinarily exchanged. Resistance to sharing things like the kind of work you do, your place of residence, your reactions to the weather, and general information on how you happen to be at the meeting are noted by others and assumed to be indicative of a desire to be left at a certain psychological distance. If the group reinforces social custom by jointly concurring on what is shared—for instance, the kind of work each one does—then it would be much more serious to hold back.

But the real question in early relationships is the extent to which you share private reactions and feelings, especially about *what is going on at the moment.* A qualitative shift in the atmosphere takes place with the sharing of private reactions, tension may mount above the conventional meeting level, and the prospects for significant interactions are increased. (For further discussion, see the section on trust and appropriate self-disclosure, p. 127.)

A special case of change in the early phases of a relationship among members of a group occurs when one or more members become silent. At first, silence may be ignored because ordinarily a reasonable margin of time is granted and a man is within his rights to come out slowly. Actually, if the silent member appears to be alert and attending to what is going on, he may be seen as an asset to the growing relationships. Many people express initial tensions by talking a lot, some by talking little.

Silence in a relationship was investigated in a laboratory setting in which two college students, strangers to each other, sat in a room but did not speak (Luft, 1966a, reproduced in these pages as Appendix 2). In this study, when a subject was asked to estimate what the other S felt toward him, the estimate was invariably similar to his own rating of the other. In other words the best indicator of what A *expects* from B is the way A *feels* toward B. Even when A's feeling toward B is not the same as B's toward A, still A's *expectation* from B is almost exactly what he feels toward B.

When B receives a response from A which is not in line with B's feelings toward A, B is placed in a state of disequilibrium about A. Equilibrium can be restored by responding in kind toward A, which increases the likelihood that B's feelings would change in a more favorable direction. In the experiment, when both S's were given spurious outside information that the ratings received were lower than those given, the initial reaction was for both to lower their liking-scores for the other. However, it did not take long for the S's, who were able to observe each other without speaking, to restore their original liking scores and even, with a bit more time, to show continued improvement in their feelings for each other. It seems reasonable to expect therefore that increased disclosure from Q3 to Q1 would be seen as an act of acceptance—unless counterindications were present—and would tend to evoke a reciprocal reaction from the other. Experimental verification of this pattern for disclosure, though not yet available so far as I know, should not be too difficult to obtain.

A classical exception to reciprocal interaction is the standard psychotherapeutic relationship in which the patient or client discloses all about himself and the therapist very little if anything. Perhaps this is the main reason for the class of events called transference or, for some therapists, increasing dependency. Currently, the trend among therapists appears to be away from this model of unilateral disclosure to a more natural interaction sequence, in which both client and therapist are more open about what is going on in their hidden quadrants. The client leads the way because it is he who comes for help. The therapist discloses his own feelings as they are relevant to and evoked by the behavior of the client.

Miscommunication

The Johari awareness model can be used to distinguish four sources of difficulty in communicating, ranging from relatively simple to more complex.

1. At the simplest level, the reason for miscommunication is lack of clarity of language. In Johari terms, the problem lies in the open quadrants of two or more persons trying to communicate with each

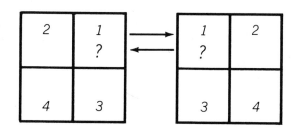

other. The communicators are seen as lacking skill in sending or receiving spoken, written, or nonverbal messages. Criticism addressed to the sender calls attention to items such as bad grammar, poor vocabulary, abuse of words and phrases and sentences, ambiguity of referents, disorderly flow of thoughts, faulty logic, redundancy, and failure to control personal idiosyncrasies at the expense of clear meaning. The receiver is held responsible for paying close attention, having an open mind, avoiding personal biases, and otherwise behaving himself so that the job of communication is not made needlessly difficult. Basic English and composition and speech courses in college and high school are concerned about this level of reading and writing, speaking and listening.

2. The problems at the second level concern the assumptions underlying the communication process. In Johari terms, two or more persons

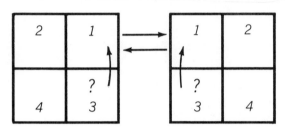

have difficulty because what is relevant and known to one or more communicators remains concealed in Q3.

> In one organization a memo was circulated about hiring a new staff member. The staff was puzzled and dismayed at this communication because the chief had not kept them informed about something as important as hiring another staff member. The chief had failed to keep his staff informed about hiring matters because his superiors up the line had held back information from *him.* A major reorganization had been considered but this change in plan was dropped; so, as far as anyone outside the policy board was concerned, things were the same as ever. But if things were the same as ever, how come staff members were not informed about such an important matter as hiring a new staff member?

Information, attitudes, and opinions remain hidden because of unfinished interpersonal work. Different or conflicting assumptions exist in the two or more persons concerned. Some way must be found for communicators to check what is going on and to make explicit what is relevant. Tacitly agreeing to disagree, if necessary, could go a long way. Providing time and support for sustaining and working on differences is, of course, important. Communication problems can be reduced by sufficient opportunities for sharing and, above all, for the development of an atmosphere of collaboration and trust. It is obvious that one can sabotage a relationship or an organization by *not* communicating. Frequently the sheer physical opportunity to swap information is not available. Formal meetings sometimes help, but the most significant Q3 sharing occurs in informal and casual settings.

For example, suppose a person voted with a majority but secretly sympathized with a minority position. Although the person is aware of his feelings on the issue at hand, he may not be aware that these feelings probably are being communicated via Q2 to others. His facial expression, tone of voice, and other nonverbal acts could send signals at variance with the explicit verbal messages. We are all guilty of sabotaging our own communication at one time or another, especially in close interpersonal relations.

3. The third level of miscommunication is as widespread as it is serious and complex. In Johari terms, Q1, Q2, and Q3 are involved simultaneously. The second quadrant is the blind one in which your

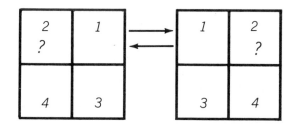

behavior, feelings, and motivation are open to others but not to you: what you do and say in Q1 may be different from and perhaps even contradictory to what others perceive in Q2. And what is hidden in Q3 further complicates the exchange.

A young minister said that it bothered him not at all to be seen in the group as a yes-man. He claimed he had his own opinions and that he did not think of himself as overly agreeable. However, the others could see that the criticism did hurt, that he was more anxious and tense under the criticism. Yet, he denied these feelings because they were in fact walled off from him. He was in no position to see and feel what others were perceiving. His communications disturbed others because they were at such variance with what they saw in his blind area. Eventually he revealed (Q3 to Q1) problems he had in his church and his sense of failure and increasing isolation. He felt that such disclosure would be devastating—but it wasn't, and he felt greatly relieved. In time he was able to express his own reactions about what was going on by acknowledging his own distress and by disclosing the ways he found to punish himself when things went wrong. He discovered that by withholding all negative feelings and showing only the positive to his congregation and to his friends, he had been signaling to them to withhold too and in the process to keep their distance. His communication problems were bound up with difficulties in appropriate disclosure, resulting in bland and distant relationships.

He had become increasingly self-critical while at the same time presenting himself as confident and self-accepting. He thought of himself as a failure but tried to act as if felt he were doing rather well. It was as if he had painted himself into a corner and was now behaving in a way which said, "This is just where I wanted to be all along and haven't I done a fine painting job on this floor."

Problems bearing on the second and third quadrants permeate all aspects of human interaction. They are mentioned briefly here in order to show a sequence of complexity in scanning the broad subject of communication.

4. The fourth level of miscommunication involves the area of unknown activity, Q4, as well as the other three quadrants. Although all quadrants are activated in any communication, each level focuses on a particular source of difficulty, as described above.

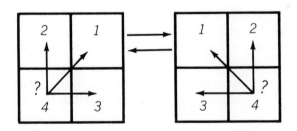

What the fourth quadrant contains is known neither to the individual nor to others, and the quadrant is known to exist only inferentially or retrospectively. Its effect on communication is thus always indirect. Behavior, feelings, and motivations may become known to others before they are known to the individual, that is, Q4 to Q2. Sometimes behavior may suddenly be clear to the individual himself, but no one else is aware of the change, so that the shift is from Q4 to Q3. What is most drastic and disconcerting is a break directly into Q1 from Q4, surprising the hell out of everyone.

Thus, the fourth level of problems is frequently concerned with intrapersonal communication. Imagination, fantasy life, daydreams, and nightdreams impinge on the individual and influence his thinking and feeling. The job of screening what comes through is perpetual; Robert Frost, for instance, refers to what comes out of working a poem as "a momentary stay against confusion" (Frost, 1949, p. vi). Unfortunately, for most of us there is not too much tolerance for primitive ideas and impulses or for crude and unsocialized feelings, even if these are merely mentioned. Art, drama, and literature help us to keep in touch with our fourth quadrants, thereby helping to sustain our inner balance if not our sanity.

The risk of being too vigilant, too early and too long, is that one may become blocked off from this part of self behind a soundproof wall. Inner communication is muffled and only the loudest cries come through. The person's communication with others loses clarity, zest, and spontaneity. To be cut off from the fourth quadrant means a decrease in the flow of ideas; imagination dries up. The literal, the conventional, and the practical take over. Change in all its forms is resisted. The capacity to grow ebbs. Communication flows as if in a concrete channel, predictable and always the same. Yet all parties concerned feel that the communication is superficial and unsatisfying.

Reestablishing contact with the fourth quadrant must be a function of change in relationships since the original difficulties took place in relation to significant others. Intrapersonal, interpersonal, intragroup (community and organization life), and intergroup relations are involved. In effect, communication at this level is altered by changes in interpersonal experience at any of the other levels discussed above. There is a wide variety of ways of looking at change and some suggestions are scattered throughout this book (see especially the section on interaction values).

Surprise is a quality associated with new interaction and fresh communication. By definition, we cannot be ready for it. Yet it may be worth reflecting on the prospect of being surprised by what comes out of our interaction with others. And we may note tendencies to avoid persons and situations which increase the probability of surprises, including both the pleasant and unpleasant varieties. Expecting the unexpected may not eliminate surprises, but it may help us to accept the prospect that sooner or later miscommunication of the Q4 variety will occur.

There are many patterns of miscommunication. An artful manipulator, for example, is one who knows that you rely on both overt and covert messages, so he manages to transmit what appear to be inadvertent Q2 communications. If you pick up the slip of the tongue or the nonverbal cue that the manipulator planted, then you may take the bait and trap yourself. As an instance, a teacher may be manipulated by a student who adopts an attentive posture and expression but whose thoughts are not on classwork.

By combining the awareness involved in Q2, Q3, and Q4 quadrants in different interaction patterns, we could hypothetically derive basic principles of miscommunication. However, we need to keep in mind that man has found ways of anticipating and discounting concealed or unknown communication by making inferences from the known to the unknown. Whether his inference system is valid or not is debatable, but there is no gainsaying that it greatly complicates an already complex enterprise.

A variant of the Q1-Q3 problem involves unverbalized expectations people have of each other as part of the interpersonal contract. There are many things left unchecked; they are simply assumed.

Two business men who have known each other a long time meet on a train leaving Vienna. "Where are you going, Herr Schmitz?" one of them asks.

"I'm going to Budapest," says Schmitz.

"Why do you lie to me, Herr Schmitz? You know very well that if you tell me you're going to Budapest I might think that you're not going to Budapest, but I happen to know that you *are* going to Budapest. Why do you lie to me?"

Privacy, Confidentialness, and Eavesdropping

The right to be left alone, the right to privacy, is a serious current issue for society and for the individual. The technology for invasion of the private realm has reached a point where conversation and behavior can be monitored at almost any time. Electronic eavesdropping has been identified by legislative and judicial experts as a threat to the individual's rights to speak out or to remain silent under the First Amendment to the Constitution.

There are many forms of persuasion and coercion that rest on invasion of privacy, so it seems ironic that one is here urged to be more revealing *in the best interests of the individual.* The nature of appropriate disclosure and the values of open communication for a person or an organization are discussed later. I should like to stress now that explorations of one's third quadrant, the hidden area, in relation to significant others is crucial to one's growth and effectiveness. But it is also important because one is strengthened in one's capacity to exercise control of disclosure and of communication by becoming better acquainted with oneself. It is not unusual in a group for participants from the same organization to discover that thoughts and feelings produced by working in the same outfit which had been locked in or censored for many years can be safely expressed. The discloser is relieved, and the persons to whom he discloses improve their understanding of him. They in turn tend to reciprocate so that communication flows more openly, candidly, and effectively. The participants find that residual feelings of misunderstanding and inadvertent distor-

53   *Quadrant 3, the Hidden Area*

tions can be more readily looked at, clarified, and dispelled. In addition, the discloser learns to discriminate more accurately what is worth disclosing.

In such a learning group, the interest is not in great personal secrets. Rather, interest focuses on the reactions going on in the group in the present. Just as others want to know how you see them so, too, are you interested in their perceptions of your behavior in the group. There appears to be universal need for occasions expressly set aside in order to look at discrepancies between the way we think and feel and the way we behave. Such experiences, openly entered into and openly pursued, have nothing in common with invasions of privacy or with eavesdropping.

Psychological researchers may inquire into one's third quadrant by means of tests, questionnaires, and physiological measuring devices. It seems to me that the same ethical considerations are involved as in eavesdropping. Does the individual know what the general purpose of the research is? Has his permission been obtained for the information? Can the subject see the general results when completed? Will his identity be protected? Will the information be treated as confidential in the way that the physician or attorney guards his client's information? Will the permission of the subject be sought before releasing data to others? These questions are only a sample of the kinds of legitimate concerns in research and testing. Perhaps the issues are obvious. At any rate they are of the greatest importance in distinguishing between invasion of privacy for external purposes and the kind of deliberate personal exploration that is essential for the individual's awareness and interpersonal effectiveness.

Parallaction

A kind of simulated interaction occurs when two or more persons appear to be undergoing an exchange but there is no involvement with each other. Perhaps we need a new term to describe this kind of parallel interaction, a process which is not covered by terms such as transaction, interaction, or even reaction. The neologism *parallaction* may be of use to describe the behavior in a relationship in which persons are in touch with one another but are acting, living, and moving independently, rather than interdependently.

Parallaction may be observed on many different occasions in a group, but particularly in the opening phases. What is going on within the total person is only superficially related to what is going on in the group. A collection of persons becomes a group when parallaction gives way to real interaction. (To grasp the enormous difference between true and simulated interaction, the reader is referred to discussions of alienation and anomie by David Riesman et al. in *The Lonely Crowd*, Martin Buber's *I and Thou*, Erich Fromm's *The Marketing Personality*, Paul Tillich's *The Courage to Be,* and Allen Wheelis' *The Quest for Identity*. However, the term parallaction as I use it refers to behavior from the simplest everyday events observable in social groups to the complex and chronic patterns of a whole culture to which some of the books refer.) In Johari terms, quadrant 1, the open area known to all, becomes enlarged. Behavior and motivation (actions and feelings) from Q3 are appropriately disclosed: brought into Q1 to form a broader basis for the emerging relationships.

Parallaction exists for a variety of reasons. Transient and ritualized business and social relationships of all kinds come to mind. The supermarket clerk and the customer ("How are you today? Bread, thirty-eight cents, milk, twenty-four cents"); the lecturer and the large class of students who never interact with each other; the physician examining a patient as if the latter were a machine in need of repairs; the husband and wife whose lives follow a parallel course, having the same interval between them during their movements, but who are living as if true interaction would only occur (to carry out the parallaction analogy) at infinity.

Other common forms of parallaction come to mind, e.g., bureau-

cratically run committees, certain families with teenagers where hom
is a place for meals and sleep and clothing storage, and certain vari
eties of courtroom procedure where interaction is controlled by stric
protocol. Note that the amount of talk is not what makes interactior
Here is a sample of parallaction that occurred in a department stor
as salesclerks stopped to chat during a lull in business.

First Clerk: How are you, Jim?
Clerk Jim: Well, better. I missed the shuttle Friday and caught a virus o
something. I've been taking those vitamin boosters and that helps bu
I have to cut down on smoking again. That tennis elbow of mine keep
me awake half the night.
First Clerk: I'm looking for Wilson; he borrowed my *Playboy* magazine.

Clerk Jim misunderstood the first clerk's intentions. Most exchange
carry an implicit agreement about the nature of the interaction. Some
times the agreement has to be made explicit when the participant
have different understandings about what is going on. Generally peopl
read each others signals very quickly. However, it is obvious that cler
Jim might easily be hurt in this simple exchange. Questions could b
raised about the background of their relationship and about the kinc
of verbal and nonverbal signals each produced and each perceivec

Self-Disclosure

You are in charge of the third quadrant, the hidden area. What yo
reveal is pretty much up to you, though not entirely so. Sometim
pressure from conflicting forces in all the quadrants forces accident
disclosure. Slips of the tongue, unusual associations of thought, ar
all kinds of mistakes may occur which reveal what you don't want

reveal. It takes energy, attention, and perhaps a good imagination to do an able job of hiding. Not disclosing could be a form of lying, obliquely by an act of omission. Selective disclosing could do a fine job of misleading, too.

William Blake wrote in his *Songs of Experience:*

A Poison Tree

I was angry with my friend:
I told my wrath, my wrath did end.
I was angry with my foe:
I told it not, my wrath did grow.

And I water'd it in fears,
Night and morning with my tears;
And I sunnèd it with smiles,
And with soft deceitful wiles.

And it grew both day and night,
Till it bore an apple bright;
And my foe beheld it shine,
And he knew that it was mine,

And into my garden stole
When the night had veil'd the pole:
In the morning glad I see
My foe outstretch'd beneath the tree.

Mowrer (1964), Jourard (1964), and Culbert (1967) find that transparency is not necessarily a mark of soundness in a person nor an indication of depth in a relationship. The key issue is appropriateness in self-disclosure, the balance of spontaneity and discretion reflecting the nature of the relationship.

Disclosing too much creates at least as many problems as disclosing too little — but of a different kind. Strict control over Q3 disclosure tends to create distance in relationships. Lax control means relationships either too close (smothering) or too demanding. The plunger, who discloses a great deal from his private, hidden sector, may be seeking to impose himself on others or may be asking others to take over control or may be wishing for closeness that is not necessarily desired by others. A child may show this most clearly. Since he has not yet developed a self strong enough and discriminating enough to cope with complex social situations, he deals with everyone by disclosing a great deal. This may be charming and enjoyable and humorous in children, but hardly so in adults.

Does self-disclosure mean the person is open, free, and trusting? Perhaps. The overdiscloser may be trying to behave openly, freely and trustingly. Or he may be unable to differentiate relationships in which such disclosure is appropriate. Superficially, he looks free and spontaneous, but he may actually be demanding more of your care, your time, and your feelings than you are prepared to offer. The over-discloser appears to trust everyone because he has not yet learned to discriminate the qualities of different relationships. It is the other person in the relationship who must take the responsibility for defining the nature of the relationship. In appropriate disclosure, behavior is reciprocal or mutual, and both persons take their proper share of responsibility for defining what the relationship is and what it is becoming.

☐ *"We do not need to reveal ourselves to others, but only to those we love. For then we are no longer revealing ourselves in order to seem but in order to give."* — Albert Camus (1963)

The underdiscloser reveals too little; he reserves control for himself. He may feel more threatened than others. His third quadrant is large and he is not moved easily to reciprocate disclosures. He is more comfortable when others disclose more than he does. He tends to quell spontaneous reactions, holding back in order to double-check what is revealed. Facial and bodily expression, the natural concomitants of feelings, are constrained to not reveal. It takes a long time to learn to mask.

The low self-discloser is preoccupied to prevent leakage from Q. He gives expressions of personal opinions and attitudes cautiously frequently using clichés and platitudes so as to avoid idiosyncrasy. He appears to be emotionally self-sufficient even when he is not. In groups, he is one of the last to recognize the development of trust. But he may be greatly surprised and relieved to find out that he can disclose more freely and more spontaneously than he imagined. It comes as a great and refreshing relief to learn that he *can* let go without being hurt and without giving up control. In exercising a bit more freedom in the group, the low self-discloser may feel as if he were being wanton and unrestrained to even admit he has feelings.

Sad to say, one sees group participants who have indeed become so impacted in Q3 that they have lost touch with themselves altogether. Only extreme feelings seem to register. When this happens, Q3 feelings and behavior may slip over into Q2 or Q4, areas unknown to the person and unavailable to him. A condition of emotional and intellectual impoverishment sets in over time. I say intellectual as well as emotional because the walling-off process does interfere with such basically intellectual resources as imagination and fantasy life.

Behavior in a learning group is inevitably a sample of one's behavior on the job or at home. Frequently, participants learn that work behavior is duplicated in the group.

A highly capable scientist discovered in the learning group his own techniques for keeping people at a distance. He was strenuously objective with everyone at all times. Recreational activities, having a beer with a colleague, even going to parties were carried out objectively and dispassionately. Although efficient as a scientist, he had become a caricature of a supervisor. Fearful that any relationship might get out of control, he had adopted the role of a perennial critic—and he was exactly the same way in the group. As the group developed and persons levelled with him about the effect he was having on them, he began to change in response to them. He was so starved for companionship that he literally cried with pleasure when he described how important the new, more open relationships in the group had become. Months after his return to his job he wrote of changes he experienced as he permitted himself more openness with his colleagues as well as with his own family. In addition, he reported that his colleagues saw him as a more effective team member as well as a more enjoyable human being.

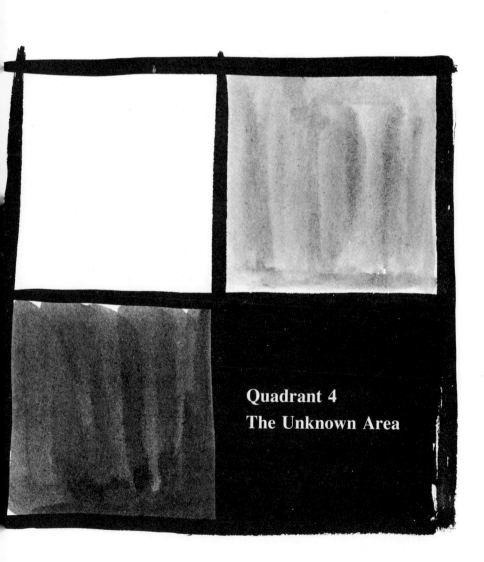

Quadrant 4
The Unknown Area

☐ *"The most beautiful experience we can have is the mysterious. It is the fundamental emotion which stands at the cradle of true art and true science. Whoever does not know it and can no longer wonder, no longer marvel, is as good as dead, and his eyes are dimmed. It was the experience of mystery — even if mixed with fear — that engendered religion. A knowledge of something we cannot penetrate, our perceptions of the profoundest reason and the most radiant beauty, which only in their most primitive forms are accessible to our minds — it is this knowledge and this emotion that constitute true religiosity; in this sense, and in this alone, I am a deeply religious man."* — **Albert Einstein,** *Living Philosophies*

Q4, the Unknown Area

What is not known to ourselves and not known to others is presumed to exist only by inference or in retrospect:

1. Confirmation after the fact is one way of identifying the existence of the unknown area.

> Andy Quivver was a reliable and pleasant staff member for a number of years. Promoted to assistant chief of the production department, Andy became a martinet, a strict, harsh disciplinarian. Since there were no other changes in his life, it was possible to identify some of the earlier docile patterns of behavior as relatable to his authoritarian ways, but no one knew it at the time, and Andy himself was not aware of it. Thus, the behavior was unknown to others and to self — until a situational change brought it out.

2. Another way of confirming the existence of Q4 is through temporary change which might occur due to the use of alcohol or drugs or during an illness. Sometimes, startling attitudes are revealed as a result of a very high fever, inebriation, or drug dosage. The individual may be surprised after recovery to hear others describe his behavior. He may be frightened, elated, or disturbed during the period of influence, and he may retain memory of specific feelings and of altered inner states after the experience. (It is doubtful that these changes provide insight, however, since a working-through stage is rarely included.)

3. Special experimental conditions such as sensory deprivation and hypnosis may also elicit behavior and memories which had been unknown to self and to others.

4. Irreversible brain injury may lead to marked changes of personality. The new pattern could then be seen as relatable to the premorbid state, though no one was aware of it before the injury.

5. Projective techniques such as the Rorschach inkblot test or the Thematic Apperception Test may reveal hidden qualities in a person which had not been suspected even by those who had known him well over time.

6. In everyday life, daydreams as well as night dreams may reveal or suggest Q4 characteristics.

☐ *"We have learned to think of knowledge as verbal, explicit, articulated, rational, logical, structured, Aristotelian, realistic, sensible. Confronted with the depths of human nature, we psychologists learn to respect also the inarticulate, the preverbal and subverbal, the tacit, the ineffable, the mythic, the archaic, the symbolic, the poetic, the esthetic. Without these data, no account of a person can possibly be complete."* — Abraham H. Maslow (1966, p. 19)

Interpersonal experiences in a group are enormously complicated by a realization of the existence of the unknown area. As the group moves through developmental states most members have an opportunity to become aware of the fourth quadrant — even if it is not brought out into Q1. Valuable experience is gained, for example, if a participant becomes newly aware of some aspect of himself heretofore unknown, as a shift occurs from Q4 to Q3.

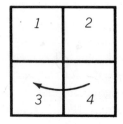

In Q3, this feeling or attitude would become known to self but not to others. The individual would thus have a choice of disclosing this new awareness or not. Heavily charged group experiences or overly dramatic events may precipitate direct disclosure to Q1 from Q4. Although some individuals could profit from such intense experience, it is generally not recommended. The pacing and timing of learning is important, and the work of a group should proceed at an optimal rather than a maximal rate. It is better to proceed out of strength and reasonable control both by the participants individually and by the group as a whole.

Groups usually tend to exercise sound judgment and to move at a reasonable speed. But it is the responsibility of the leader to exercise discretion for the simple reason that the number of unknowns in any group is so very large. Group pressure can be an overwhelming lever to move some persons before they are really ready. Even though protective resources exist in the individual and in the group, there is no point in taxing these resources to the limit. One disadvantage of going beyond anyone's psychological reserves is that the experience may set the group back in its explorations and discoveries by frightening some members and immobilizing others.

Understanding Q4 functions in the total picture is important because in everyday life there is obviously the same kind of problem. Relationships within organization are often so complex and intense and so resistant to rational, logical approaches that they clearly suggest the presence of deeply hidden and unknown areas of behavior. The size of quadrant four in relation to the other quadrants is not directly knowable, but it is much larger than the area usually indicated. For the sake of simplicity, the model is ordinarily shown as divided into four equal quadrants.

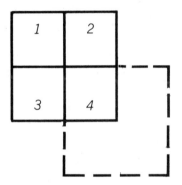

I do not suggest that persons in social or industrial organizations attempt to deal in some direct fashion with the blind quadrant, Q4. It may be enough for a beginning to know of the quadrant's existence. The Johari awareness model may thus be useful in providing a way of thinking about and talking about the unknown quadrant of behavior. Since every individual and group has unknown areas, Q4 offers an approach to the appreciation of atypical and deviant behavior which might otherwise be thought of as mental illness. A language and vocabulary of interpersonal behavior is preferable because it is less misleading than the language of psychopathology. The latter is the language of medicine and the physician; it invokes implicitly a physicalistic theory of behavior. The Johari concept rests on a number of broad assumptions, described early in this book, supporting the idea that personality *is* one's interpersonal patterns of behavior and is acquired through life by psychosocial learning. In the latter context, behavioral unknowns are less apt to be seen as alien to the person.

Potential for the Future, Residue of the Past

Quadrant four contains the untapped resources of the person. What we inherit in our genes and what remains as yet unrealized is an important component of quadrant four. Latent talent may grow at any time in life depending on conditions and opportunities. People may bloom with extraordinary abilities in their later years, and as the life span is extended more persons have the opportunity to develop their Q4 resources.

The residue of past experience is also contained in Q4. Perhaps it is true that whatever has registered with us once psychologically may be assumed to exist in the unknown quadrant. Robert Frost has said, "The impressions most useful to my purpose seem always those I was unaware of and so made no note of at the time when taken" (Frost, 1949, p vii). Sometimes unusual or dangerous events activate memories long thought to be forgotten. There are many experiments, especially in hypnosis, in which large segments of experience are recalled almost intact.

Of particular importance are the difficult past experiences of the person against which strong defenses had to be built. Everyone does this—but at a price. The price is a walling off of the traumatized area, and this may cause impacting of all kinds of resources. New experience, new sensations, and new learning may be impeded or avoided because they are too close to what has been quarantined. Anxiety warns the individual not to risk the new for fear of re-arousing the old hurt. Each of us owes some of our uniqueness to these buried experiences. But there is no need to be hobbled to be unique. As a matter of fact, with the release and development of more of our resources, we can be even more idiosyncratic, more individual. Uniformity of persons comes about through social molding to a common pattern.

It is axiomatic that with greater exercise of the individual's psychological resources, variety and diversity *increase*. The individual has more choice. He has more depth of feeling, more shades of experience. He has access to more associations of thought and in greater combination. He may suffer doubts where others have none. His inner richness opens him to all kinds of human states with one possible exception: he emigrates away from a feeling of certainty. He can at the same time be more self-confident because he is more open to and aware of the realities of his human environment.

Awareness and Experience

Much of what we know we cannot describe, e.g., walking, talking with a child, reading, writing, recognizing our own bodies, the appearance and posture of a friend (see Polanyi, 1958, for more detailed instances). The paradox is that we know more than we are aware of knowing. What we learn is more than a set of discrete elements. Only the less important things are learned by specific points, such as how to run a slide rule or an automatic washer. But how do we learn to enjoy a friendship, to see a play, to share responsibility on a job? Learning occurs of course through direct, inexplicit experience as well as by explicit awareness.

Although behavior and feelings may be identified principally with one quadrant, all four quadrants are involved and affected in each act. Writing a letter is an example of a first quadrant event, but one in which the whole person may be touched.

It is equally true that when I read a letter all four quadrants are involved and I am affected by what is communicated. I may be reminded of things I had forgotten. I may interpret the letter in terms of what I see in my correspondent's Q2. I may be puzzled by an indirect manifestation in the letter of feelings coming from the writer's Q4. My own fourth quadrant may be stimulated as I read the letter, but I do not then fully understand my own reaction. I may also have information or feelings (Q3) which I have not shared with my correspondent but which have an effect on *me* as I read the letter.

In the same way, an act that does not involve words may affect us totally. Thus change and growth are potentially derivable from experience. This point is emphasized because reading and writing about feelings-in-relationships tend to dwell on cognitive or intellectural knowing. Verbalizable insight is important, but not the main goal. Learning in groups is essentially learning through experience, but learning by verbalizable knowledge drawn from experience also occurs.

☐ *"What is so unusual about this lab is all this attention to feeling. It's made me do a lot of thinking."* — Participant in a learning laboratory ‖

In a group, talking about group processes is not the same as experiencing them. Nor is talk about interpersonal relationships necessarily involved in experiencing such relationships. To be in a group and to *experience* a process (such as evasion, acceptance, scapegoating, collusion) and to be able to *observe* it and *talk* about it as well, is a powerful way to learn of human interaction.

One of the values of group interaction is the discovery that certain alternatives are open to us of which we were not aware.

A young psychiatrist in one lab group learned something about his lack of interpersonal effectiveness. Though he had become aware of the fact that his contributions to the group were generally ignored, he was unaware of his tendency to defuse his remarks by a rather apologetic way of expressing himself. When the effect of his manner on others was pointed out he began to realize that this was a residual behavior pattern from the past no longer applicable to the present. In a relatively short time he found he could dispense with some of the older patterns and assert himself in a more direct way. Individually he reflected on the sources of his overly qualified manner, but within the group he realized that he could, if he wanted, express himself more directly. His subjective explorations were stimulated by the group's reaction to him and he found himself privately examining other areas of his life and finding fresh leads to work on. In short, the process of learning continued with this psychiatrist outside of the group between meetings, and may well have continued after he left the lab.

Participants are generally capable, normal, and rather highly motivated persons. Ordinarily, persons with severe personality disorders are not encouraged to participate in these learning experiences, although there is little doubt that under the right conditions, they too can take advantage of lab learning. Maxwell Jones' phrase "therapeutic community" refers to a group in interaction that has many qualities and characteristics of a human relations laboratory. For example, Jones and Paul Polak describe a crisis as "an intolerable situation which threatens to become a disaster or calamity if certain organizational and psychological steps do not take place immediately" (Jones and Polak, 1968). The authors propose a face-to-face confrontation with crisis participants led by a professional skilled in group methods, in a setting that encourages communication of feelings.

However, under no circumstances is lab learning of the sort discussed in these pages to be viewed as a shortcut to mental health. There are mental health practitioners in private practice as well as in public institutions who should be consulted for psychological or psychiatric assistance. But certainly there is a need by persons who are functioning well and who might in many respects be stronger and more capable than average to have access to special learning resources. Students, teachers, business people, managers, supervisors, doctors, psychologists, engineers, clergymen, housewives, union people, executives, nurses, public health specialists, artists, technicians, professors, and personnel workers have for the last two decades participated in such groups with sufficient personal and professional benefit to encourage others to attend. Many in fact have returned to the various encounter groups conducted by the National Training Laboratories and by universities and other educational institutions around the country for a second or a third experience in interpersonal learning.

The Participant-Observer

Observation can give facts, raw sense data, the *sine qua non* of scientific method. Observing behavior in a group looks deceptively easy. But so much is going on at once and so many things compete for the observer's attention. Observation is a function of the observer, a part of his personality. What he sees or hears or feels is always selective and is determined in large part by what is going on in him as well as by what is taking place around him (see Kaplan, 1964).

Raw sense data may not be easy to relate to specific qualities. Apples look like apples, and that may be good enough. You may buy some apples because the look of them tells you that they will be crisp and juicy and taste slightly sour. I may decline to buy because to me they look overripe and too mealy. We each try one of those you bought and discover that we both like them, but for taste qualities neither of us expected.

Observing and experiencing apples is complicated enough (regardless of who pays for them), but interacting with people and observing people is truly formidable (see H. C. Smith, 1966).

Can skill in observation be learned? I think so. There are several important guides to be noted briefly:

1. Observation starts with one's self. The greater congruence between your feelings and your own behavior, the better your prospects for observing others.

2. The good observer has a large first quadrant, and the other quadrants are relatively smaller than for most persons. Conflicts in the areas unknown to the observer are not so strong or active that they color all his observations. Some paranoid patients, for example, may be keen observers of certain parts of their environment, but the meaning to them is frought with suspicion, doubt, and danger. The latter qualities stem from deep and long standing difficulties buried in Q2, Q3, and Q4.

3. The good observer has had broad and varied experience. That is, he has observed and experienced all kinds of people and events and these are plausible even if not entirely understood. He appreciates varieties of personality and differences in cultural practice even if such variations are not always pleasant or entirely comprehended. His Q1 is large enough to encompass great ranges of human conduct, differences, and atypicallity.

4. The practice of taking more than one sample of a particular slice of behavior is valuable. Everyone talking at once in a group can mean all kinds of things. One might observe the faces and bodies of the participants, what they are saying, how they are saying it, who is talking to whom, who is being ignored, what went on just before, etc. Without forcing a fit, the observer can look at the different data samples. Can they be fitted together in different patterns? How many alternative hypothesis can be generated?

5. Tentative observation calls for an ability in the observer to reserve judgment till more information is gathered. I don't think one can really stop judging, but I do think it is possible to learn to try out many different hunches before zeroing in.

6. Generating alternative hunches and searching for additional ideas that fit are important values. I emphasize the search for alternatives because even a half-formed idea forces you to look for new evidence.

7. Theories about behavior and interaction are fundamental to observation. Knowledge of several theories of human behavior is important because each theory applies best to a particular realm of behavior. Miniature or subtheories are valuable; I refer to limited sets of ideas such as one on varieties of humor or on apathy. A rich theory, one with which you've had lots of practice and which has broad generalizability, is like a powerful flashlight. Theories generate hypotheses and

ideas; they help you ask yourself questions, and questions are the probes searching out the human environment.

8. Your feelings are the main guide in observation. It's not so much what you see that counts, it's what you see-and-feel. You may feel what others are feeling (your feeling tense makes me feel tense, your feeling cheerful makes me feel cheerful). Or you may feel the effects of what others are expressing (your feeling helpless brings out protective feelings in me).

9. Intuition is essentially a matter of feeling. A slight or marginal feeling may steer your attention and your thinking toward hitherto unseen behavior—sudden insights may seem to occur out of the blue. Seemingly unrelated bits of behavior fall into place. But intuition and insight are not accidental phenomena. Like most good ideas or inventions, behavioral insights occur most often to those who are industriously and intimately involved, informed, and ingenious.

Learning groups emphasize participation *and* observation. Splitting these functions is commonplace as in viewing television or passive participation in company politics. Vicarious participation is a safer form of participation. Looking without doing may be enjoyable and deeply moving, but behavioral learning calls for action.

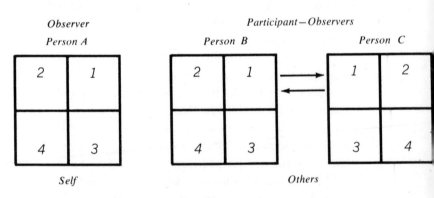

Person *A* observed *B* and *C* interacting (e.g., as on television). *A* may be affected by what he sees, but he is not seen and he cannot influence the interaction. *B* and *C* are each observing and participating in the action. They may be aware of *A's* observing (as in live drama) but they have no idea or limited clues (clapping) of what is going on with *A*. Yet even limited clues such as restlessness, silence, laughing may affect the performers vitally.

Some people work in groups as if they were watching television; they may not be able to change channels but the switch can be turned off. In every group, office, school, shop, family, and committee, someone is silently disconnected. He does not hear or see what is going on around him; he phases in and out. Check this with the people in your next meeting, wherever it is. Better yet, check yourself. / / /

The participant-observer learns to do just that—to check his participation and his observation. With the help of others, you may learn to be a bit more observant of your own observation skill and of your participation as well. You might try deliberately not observing yourself, and then try checking with others afterward to see how their observations fit with the feel of your own participation.

One responsibility of the leader and eventually of the other participants in a learning group is to provide simple occasions which are fresh and new for the participants so that they may enjoy seeing themselves perform unpracticed behavior. Greeting each other without words was useful in one group; another group came up with a suggestion to build a dam in a nearby stream. A few minutes of play-acting was useful in another group when one of the members told of his annoyance with a traffic cop who had given him a ticket. Someone in the group suggested he demonstrate by playing the policeman as well as himself. The simulated participation was revealing to the group observers as well as to the main actor.

Self-Report

During encounter group sessions participants are sometimes encouraged to keep a log or diary. In a group process class, students may be asked to write weekly reports or term papers. Here are excerpts from reports turned in by students writing as participant-observers.

I am developing a more vivid self-awareness. I've been aware of certain of my reaction patterns but I am amazed to see myself demonstrate them so automatically and consistently. For example, theoretically I believe spontaneous behavior is desirable; however, when one member attacks another, or expresses a "dangerously" sensitive feeling, I find myself attempting either verbally or nonverbally to minimize the contribution and help return the group atmosphere to a more controlled and nonthreatening situation.

After thinking about it a little more, I realize now why I struck back at the boy who accused me of being too "wordy." I simultaneously was insulted, but also realized somewhere in my mind that unknowing to this boy he had seen through the very slight role I was playing. I'm not sure he was conscious of it, but I was. I was trying to impress the group with my sophistication, my poise and reassurance, choosing each word carefully, not speaking too rapidly. He had destroyed my self-image just a little and I hated him for it.

Although we talked about how many "nice manners" — nauseatingly so — were being displayed, some of these have dropped by the wayside. There seems to be some process of dropping the masks with some of the members of the group. But we seem to me to not yet be a "group." For instance, we can't seem to get off the ground with any "ideas" — partly because the instructor brings us back by asking someone, "How did you feel when they were talking about this," or "while this interaction was taking place."

Where fourteen people once sat rather staidly with a somewhat detached coolness, we now seem to have changed our overt *postural* habits, exhibiting with fluidity and change the feelings and reactions we feel as they become more or less intense with the subject at hand. Mary, for example, no longer sits straight and cool in her chair but last week with vigor and exasperation ran her hand through her hair as though she was symbolically pulling it out in frustration when a conversational exchange disturbed her. I think all of us have shown varying degrees of change in our postural participation.

For the past two months I have been very confused and upset because I felt I wasn't learning anything. All of a sudden this past week the "light" finally dawned. I have learned something, and I've learned quite a bit. I've learned how to be a group member. Why I couldn't see it before I'll never know. I've learned through personal participation what it feels like to be angry with another member of the group, how to respond to criticism, how to watch for verbal communication, how to destroy a group's cohesion, what it feels like to be confused and left-out, what boredom or disinterest is. All of these are just a few of the many things I unconsciously have been learning all along. But one of the most startling realizations is that quite possibly I am a coward. The small caucus we had in class this week made me realize that in class I am often more concerned with what other people will think of me than I am of my convictions. If I think other members of the group will think I am "stupid" if I make a certain remark, I will most probably avoid making it.

The most significant processes that have been taking place, especially last Thursday, for me boils down to one word, which may then be used as a starting place for different subprocesses. The essence of these subprocesses is "discovery." In that room last Thursday there were so many discoveries taking place, discoveries that may prove extremely meaningful for different members of the group.

Firstly, there was the finding that your private emotional or psychological ache or hurt is not a commodity on which one person has rights. The fact is and this came out last week, we *all* are hurt. Concomitant with this realization, came the process of discovering that when you are hurt by another, that other person may not even *know* he hurt you—and in fact, the probability may be that there are more cases of unintentional than intentional hurting of another. If you've never known this before, what a wonderful discovery!

Thirdly, came the finding that other people have aches and hurts about which we know nothing! We assume that their calm face represents a calm collection of feelings, but the fact was revealed last week that this may not necessarily be the case at all! And along with this came the discovery that *you* in fact may have been responsible for hurting someone without ever realizing it. And this kind of realization, or insight, or what-have-you, can bring intense sadness—for if you don't *know* and are not *told,* there is nothing you can do to ease the pain you've caused someone.

The process of discovering *these* things, led to more. For one thing, it showed some of us that feelings of uneasiness in your relationship with another may well have some basis. And more important, that to explore these feelings (i.e., of uneasiness) may cause their eventual dissipation! What a wonderful thing to learn! Fear then of what *may* be, can be destroyed by the learning of what *is.*

Group Interaction

Group Interaction

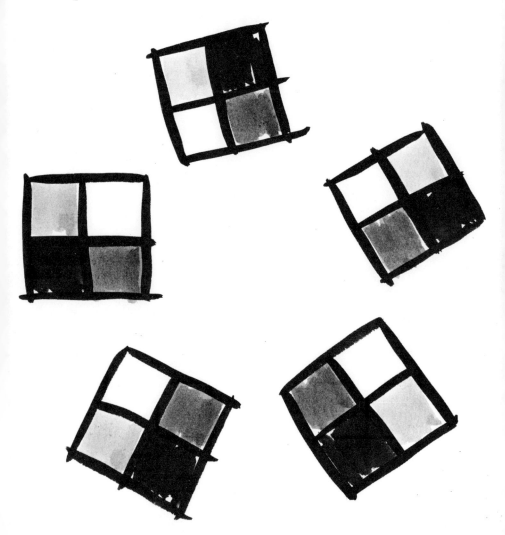

Reasons for Coming Together

In an encounter or laboratory group on human learning, "What am I doing here?" is a question more often felt than heard. There are good reasons and real reasons, practical reasons and impractical ones, known reasons and unknown reasons. Here are some typical responses when the question is voiced:

"I want to learn about groups."

"I'll be darned if I know. Everybody's going and I guess I'm just curious."

"My wife thinks it will do me a lot of good."

"I'm thinking of changing jobs and maybe this will help me figure out what I want to do."

"I'm a minister and I'm dissatisfied with the response of my congregation."

"I want to learn how to handle a few guys in my outfit."

"I want to see if this will be useful in my organization. We're in trouble and I'm willing to try anything at this point."

"I'm a loner in my company and in my personal life. I want to change that."

"I like people and I find groups exciting."

"I'm tired of being pushed around. I want to learn how to do some pushing of my own."

"I get along fine with people. Only thing I want to know is what they really think of me."

"It will help me in my career."

"I want to learn how to communicate better, that's all."

I think that this is not an unfair sample. The stated responses tell part of the story, but not the whole story by any means. It is perfectly understandable that most of the reasons are partial and provisional: reasons change as things start happening, and what happens can be predicted only in a rather broad sense. The essence of the experience depends on the particular members of the group and, to a considerable extent, on the leader and the group context. A college setting for a college course in group processes will be different from a group made up of managers within a company. And a leader who is trained and oriented in group processes will influence the group differently than will one whose interest and specialization is in the field of mental health.

Nevertheless, a well-run group does go through certain recognizable stages regardless of the identity of the members or the particular setting. It may be of interest to participants in a human relations lab to learn that when staff members get together before the lab begins, they too go through these same stages regardless of their previous experience and their expertise with groups.

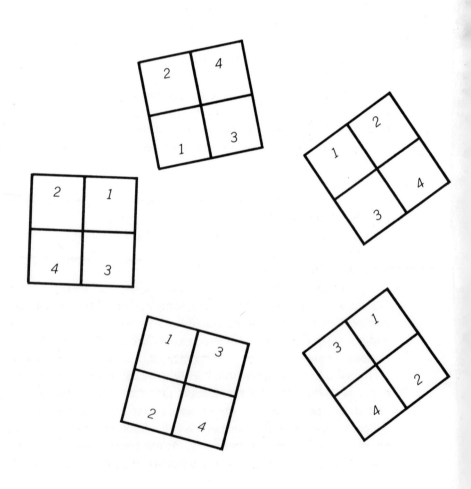

Interaction between Groups

Groups have wholeness properties. A family, for example, can be described as a unit. So can a company, a club, an office staff, a gang, a community. Groups can be arranged in terms of values, goals, or functions or whatever it is that binds members to each other. There is no limit to the kinds of properties or classifications by which groups may be described.

	Known to group	Not known to group
Known to other groups	1	2
Not known to other groups	3	4

The Johari awareness model of the group as a whole
in relation to other groups

In some ways groups behave like individuals, e.g., talkative families or disorganized communities or biased clubs. Just about any quality ascribed to an individual may be ascribed to a group. But it may not always be useful to do so.

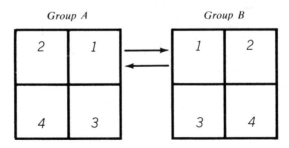

Interaction between two groups

Groups develop lives of their own and ways of their own. An important group quality is the extent to which the members are aware of the behavior and feelings of the group as a whole.

Groups interact with other groups in an arena of openness that is less than the total area of behavior and attitudes known to the group. Some knowledge of behavior or attitude remains hidden (Q3), and some behavior and feeling of the group is inaccessible to the group but may be known to other groups so that it is in the blind quadrant (Q2). In short, the Johari model may be applied to *intergroup* relationships.

When groups get into difficulty, when they bog down and fail to meet the individual or collective needs of the membership, there is a universal tendency to search for explanations at the individual level. The tendency to blame individual members is so strong that it makes other approaches difficult to consider. Nonetheless, the model of the group as a whole suggests that the sources of difficulty may be within the functioning of the entire group. (The analogy of a family in which only one member seems to be troubled comes to mind. Nowadays, a child or other family member with problems is apt to be thought of in terms of difficulties within the family and not in terms of the child's intrapsychic life alone.)

Groups interacting with groups are much more apt to respond to each other according to group properties rather than to qualities of individual members. Interaction between the rich and the poor, blacks and whites, the old and the young, and so on may best be understood in terms of the images these groups have of each other. The use of a sterotype tells us that the user's perception is limited, incomplete, and distorted. The Johari model points out that the behavior and attitudes of any two groups are partially open, partially blind, partially hidden, and partially unknown. The relationship between the groups depends on the ways and means they develop to change the states of awareness and unawareness within and between them.

In his *Civilization and Its Discontents*, Freud talks of the "narcissism of minor differences" between groups. He had in mind the competitive and hostile feelings that so often exist between fairly close groups such as the Spanish and the Portuguese, the North and the South Germans.

It is not easy to understand or appreciate the ways of other groups. Getting outside of one's group or one's culture is not a bad way to learn about one's own ways. In ordinary intergroup relations, however, opportunities to learn about how the others see your group are not easily created.

Exchanges between groups are only a beginning in helping groups grow in awareness of selves and others. Even more important than the simple exchange of views between groups is the development of relations to a point that the processes of give and take, of impression and feedback, may be sustained. And here again we return to the problems of developing acceptance and trust, and the ways of enlarging the view each group has of itself and of the other.

Trapped in Games without End — 1

Within every group lies the prospect of blocking itself into a genuine stalemate. Left alone a group may work out of a stalemate, thereby enhancing its own growth and autonomy. But not all groups can free themselves from the bind of their own implicit rules. There are families, groups and organizations locked for years in traps of their own making. One can see some of these snares working in groups designed to learn about groups.

The leader's interventions stem from his freedom not to be bound by the hidden rules; thus he is able to offer an opportunity to the group to move outside of its system. This principle, which has grown out of work with normal populations in encounter groups and college classes, fits precisely the experience of other specialists in interpersonal relations. Halpern (1965, p. 177) states that "for psychotherapy to succeed the therapist must avoid becoming unwittingly ensnared in the disturbance-perpetuating maneuvers of his patient." Beier in his discussion of the information-gathering process in psychotherapy (1966, p. 43) observes that "his (the therapist's) measurements are his sensitivity to covert cues and his skill in disengaging from the social involvement which the patient tries out with him." Laing (1961, p. 21) finds that "his ability to shake off the 'reality' imposed by the group is the essential task of the group analyst."

Watzlawick, Beavin, and Jackson (1967, p. 234) identify the very same principle in their work with families. Unless the therapist stays sufficiently outside the rules and assumptions governing their interaction patterns, "we have the whole group snared in games without end." They use the term "games" in the sense of von Neumann's conception as later modified by Szasz (1961) and by Berne (1961 and 1966): the creation of a relatively closed, implicit, interactional system regulating how people perceive each other. A "game without end" is one in which the prospect of working out of a bind is effectively blocked by an implicit or explicit rule. For example, if a group has a rule which states that every decision must be endorsed unanimously, no action is possible when real differences occur. Further, it is not possible to change the rule since it requires unanimous agreement, and the minority group will not permit the change. Such entrapment in a game without end can be broken only if rules are changed to permit decisions even when differences cannot easily be resolved. Decisions by simple majority vote could of course also interfere with group functioning unless provision is made for protection of minorities and the creation of machinery for the resolution of differences.

Trapped in Games without End — 2

Every relationship generates its own rules. Every family, every friendship, every group lives by a set of guidelines which are implicit, in addition to those which are explicit. The explicit rules are more amenable to understanding and therefore are much less difficult to live with and to change.

A new group quickly sets up its own rules, procedures, and structure even if these are loose and informal. Participants usually bring in rules—including implicit rules—from past experience. These rules may facilitate coming to terms, initially, with others. Occasionally the rules and the system of interaction that evolves produce disturbances which interfere with learning or with other work.

The group, in a human relations lab for instance, has considerable leeway to ensnare itself and to work out of its own traps. In doing so the group sets up new rules to replace the old. Finally, the group runs into a crisis. Its machinery for modifying rules and changing the system breaks down. Or the system of rules may have a limit which is fixed and this limit now blocks change.

A group split on an important issue. Strong feelings were aroused pro and con but neither side would budge. A suggestion was made that each person write out anonymously personal impressions about what was causing the crisis and these would be collected in a copper vase that happened to be handy. When all the slips of paper were collected, the leader, who had made the suggestion, set down the vase and asked the group what they wanted done with the collection. A number of suggestions were made but each was vetoed. _There was no mechanism for making a group decision._ Some participants wanted their slips read, others demurred and said it would reflect on the ones who chose not to. The discussion went on for two whole days. Every existing rule was tried but none covered this situation. The implicit rules were gradually made explicit, but even these did not cover the contingency. How do you arrive at consensus when there is no agreement on arriving at consensus? By the end of the second day, the group had so thoroughly examined the way it functioned that it had exhausted all interest in the notes sitting in the copper vase. The members revealed far more than they put down on paper. They learned something about the ways they used to block people who differed with them. They learned that consensus by simple majority vote doesn't always work, and that it was far more valuable to search for the understanding behind the vote. They began to realize that their behavior in this crisis was similar to their behavior outside the group. But "back home" the crisis was never pushed to its limits and allowed to play itself out. Also, the group had the luxury of time to look at what was happening and to invent ways of helping to achieve understanding.

If the leader had permitted himself to enter the system as a member he too would have been trapped. He realized, perhaps intuitively, that it was essential to get outside of the rules and the system, and the way he did so was to propose the copper vase as a new kind of communications channel. When the participants realized that the control over this channel represented control over the group, they fought and successfully blocked every way out. Only then did they realize the nature of their dilemma and stumble onto the new way. The new way was to permit exploration of hidden and indirect reasons for behaving the way they did. They learned about the relationship between the need to control the group and trust. They became more aware of how trust was gained and the anxiety it cost. They also found out about the covert collusion within subgroups to block action and decision.

The leader could of course have been any other member of the group. Often a participant will rescue a group and its designated leader who has himself become trapped in the implicit rules of the system. It is easy to see how any leader could become trapped in games without end. The leader has his own tendencies to generate implicit and ensnaring rules. Also, it is essential that he follow very closely what is going on in the group, so that he gets a feel of the strivings and conflicts involved. But to the extent that he does permit himself to become involved in the life of the group, he may become ensnared in its games, and to that extent he loses effectiveness.

The major technique for helping a group to learn about its stalemate is to provide a channel or a process that is not covered by the implicit rules and assumptions. Sometimes this is done by asking, in one way or another, that the group look at its own functioning. Calling attention to an ongoing process brings into awareness (Q1) something which the group could not see (Q2) or something they preferred not to see (Q3). Either sort of disclosure may help the group to find a way to escape the entrapping game.

Bennis gives a psychodynamic rationale for the kind of entrapment that so often arises in encounter or T-groups (1964):

> In the second subphase counterdependent members begin to rebel against the leader. They may criticize him obliquely or openly; they may ignore him or lead him to give opinions only to prove him wrong. Or they may oust him. The secret wish for his omnipotent protection remains but now *this* aspect is in abeyance. The atmosphere of the group is one of disappointment, hostility, suspicion of his motives and rebellion.

The behavior of a participant can inform you whether for him it is a Q2 or a Q3 function. For the participant who is blind to the process, the intervention of the leader is seen either as a stroke of genius if the participant is ready for the insight, or, if he is not yet ready, as irrelevant. (I am assuming, of course, that the leader is on target.) The participant for whom the process is a Q3 event reacts to the intervention as if he were suddenly exposed, caught red-handed.

Another class of interventions, referred to as structural interventions (see Appendix 1), requires that the leader be aware of the need to break through an unprofitable game set in which the group is engaged. When it is successful, the structural intervention helps to make explicit the limiting implicit rules. The group may not always accept an intervention by the leader—or by any of its members for that matter. The leader's influence will vary with the group, his approach and style, and the time spent together, among other things. It may well be that optimal effectiveness is limited to a relatively short period of time. After that the leader himself begins to be bound in by the implicit rules and members are freer to accept or reject anyone's special influence.

The Floogle

Collecting floogles is neither a hobby nor an avocation. Experts in the field claim that those who collect floogles (called flooglers) have a tendency to floogle quite a bit themselves. Floogle is a verb: I floogle, you floogle, he, she, or it floogles. Yet it is also a noun, as in, I just made a floogle. Floogles can be found everywhere, but good floogles are hard to come by. They are swift and elusive, and it takes experience to spot a floogle in the making.

Here are a few in my collection:

1. After a long silence in one group, a member stated, "This has been such a comfortable silence I felt no need to break it."

2. In the middle of a disagreement with another member, a participant slammed his hand on the table and said, "I will *not* let this stupid argument get me mad."

3. A minister in a group was being heckled by another group member who accused all clergymen of being somewhat paranoid. The minister said the charge was ridiculous. He claimed he had heard similar name calling before, and ended by saying, "I'm getting sick and tired of this kind of talk. Why in the world do people keep picking on *us?*"

4. The leader in a group was being severely censured by one of the group members for expressing his opinion. "As the leader of this group you have no right to criticize or to judge," he was told. "Just reward those who are doing the right thing."

5. During a staff meeting, one leader criticized several of his colleagues for suggesting ideas for a lab design in which certain specific activities were to be scheduled. "I want to object to this design," he said with considerable vigor, "I will not stand by and take this point of view. You and you and you," he added, pointing to three of the staff members, "are trying to *make* things happen in a group and my philosophy is to *let* things happen."

As you can see, there is quite a bit of variation in these floogles, and as an amateur floogler I'm rather proud to have them in my collection.

In Johari terms, a floogle is a Q2-Q1 event. For instance, at the moment of occurrence the person who said angrily that he is not getting mad is unaware of the contradiction between what he thinks he is saying and what gets communicated. Each bit of behavior, both

1 I won't get mad	*2* I'm getting mad
3	*4*

A floogle

verbal and nonverbal, serves to express some aspect of the individual's mixed feelings. It is clear that the nonverbal content in Q2 in this case reveals more accurately the state of affairs of which the person himself is, at that instant, unaware. This Q2 behavior (banging the table or raising his voice) could be pointed out to him, and he may or may not acknowledge the discrepancy. However, what is particularly interesting about a floogle is that frequently no one among the listeners recognizes a true floogle just as it is being made.

Psychodrama

A psychodrama is a form of role-playing in which participants interact as if they were different persons or themselves in different circumstances. The aim of psychodrama is to increase awareness (enlarging Q1) and to encourage spontaneity by play-acting conflicts. It should be noted that role-playing can generate a heavy flow of unproductive anxiety unless properly carried out. The selection and arrangement of a psychodrama should depend on the specific problem, the particular persons involved, and the context of the relationships.

Many varieties of psychodrama are possible. The following descriptions give a few of the more important kinds of role-playing in Johari terms.

1. Persons *A* and *B* play the roles of supervisors *C* and *D*. While the *C* and *D* roles are interacting, *A* and *B* are of course interacting

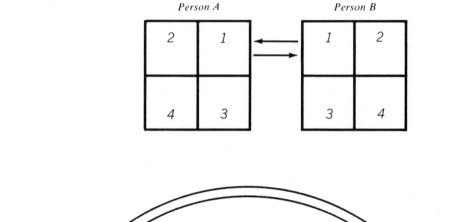

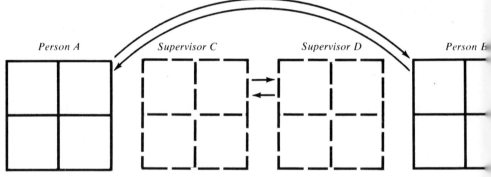

too. The psychodrama may provide an aid to learning about the relationships of:

Persons *A* and *B*	Person *A* and dyad (*B* and *C*)
Supervisors *C* and *D*	Person *A* and dyad (*B* and *D*)
Person *A* and supervisor *C*	Person *B* and dyad (*A* and *C*)
Person *A* and supervisor *D*	Person *B* and dyad (*A* and *D*)
Person *B* and supervisor *C*	Person *A* and self
Person *B* and supervisor *D*	Person *B* and self

The group (*A*, *B*, *C*, and *D*)

2. Person *A* plays *A* but *B* role-plays someone else, *C*.

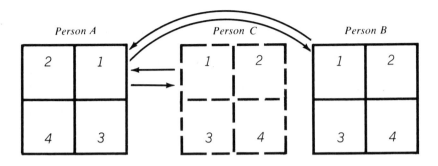

3. Person *A* plays *A* but *B* role-plays part of *A*. In the illustration, *B* plays the specific role of *A's* censor, as once happened in a group.

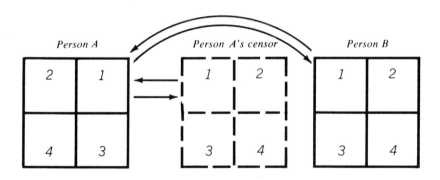

The reason for selecting *A's* censor as the role concerned *A's* inter-action with the group in which he revealed that he occasionally did censor his own behavior unnecessarily and that he wanted to under-stand this better. *B's* portrayal of *A's* censor, of course, reflects *B's* perception of *A*. *B's* perception of *A* may be as revealing of *B* as it is of *A*.

4. Person *A* plays two roles, each a different aspect of self. In this drama, *A* plays *A1* and *A2*, trying in each case to portray his thoughts and feelings in line with the role. In the illustration, the two roles are

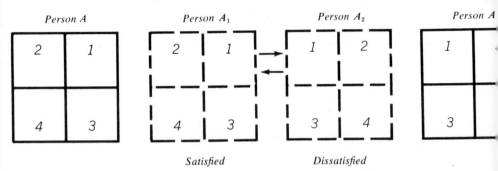

of satisfaction with self and dissatisfaction with self. There may be differences in voice, language, and content as well as differences in the feelings expressed in the two roles. *A's* conflict with self becomes the focus of the interaction, and the role-play may help *A* to clarify for himself something of the nature of the conflict.

5. The entire group participates, role-playing an event, a problem or a happening. The drama might be framed around an event that had

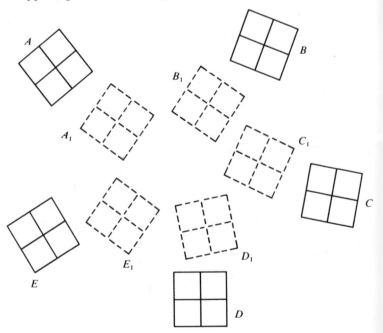

occurred in the group, or about a problem found to be difficult or puzzling. It might start deliberately with one member assuming a role and others joining in whenever they feel like it and then taking whatever role they choose. The drama moves toward a crisis point and soon afterward the action might be halted. Then each member reverts to his usual self and talks about what he observed and felt in the play.

There are innumerable forms of psychodrama; they may refer to ongoing group life, job situations, back-home problems, or future events. Like other techniques, psychodrama is only as useful as the skill and experience of the leader and participants permit. It is usually guided by improvisation for the best fit to what is salient at the time. Simple, brief plays are best; complex situations and props are typically less productive. The state of affairs in the group, the nature of relationships and the strengths, weaknesses, and difficulties of the various participants need to be taken into account. Because role-playing can stimulate regressive tendencies and loosen psychological controls, it is obviously important to understand the function of these processes in relation to problem-solving, anxiety production, and growth needs.

Research Applications

The Johari model lends itself to systematic inquiry into group, organizational, and interpersonal behavior. Data may be gathered for each quadrant, depending on the theoretical question under investigation. Some problems may center on the differences in quadrant size for different populations or for different situations. Normative estimates may be made of "openness" in Q1, for example, in the usual psychometric ways. Samples of the universe of behavior between students and teachers, between managers and supervisors, or between scientist colleagues, etc., could be collected. Following standardization procedures, the investigator could establish acceptable levels of reliability and validity in the usual manner. Sidney Jourard's instrument for measuring self-disclosure (1964, pp. 160-64) seems to be of this nature.

The blind area, Q2, would appear to be a promising field for inquiry. In an organization, for instance, it should be possible to gather data on behavior known to *A, B, C, D,* and *E,* but not to *F.* To what extent, for example, is a supervisor aware of behavior and motivation known to his subordinates but not to him about his relationship with them? To what extent do subgroups exist based on differences in the way they perceive the organization or its power structure? In a school, hospital, government agency, industrial plant, university, or neighborhood, studies could be designed to look at discrepancies in perception of revelant behavior within the organization, among its subunits, and between it and other organizations.

In one study, Jay Hall has made a highly interesting research application of the Johari model. When his standardization data has been completed, he and his associates will have a basis to make a number of useful applications. In particular his interpretation of interpersonal climates and quality of relationship based on quadrant size and shape are original and exciting uses of the model. His ideas on the "overuse and underuse" of processes (feedback and openness) develop out of his particular theory of management and follow his scheme for quantifying the Johari quadrants.

I should explain that I make quite a case for the "overuse and underuse" of processes when I present the Johari and I try to get people to think in terms of the consequences of both for interpersonal climates. In effect, I coordinate the overall *size* of the Arena to the quantitative productivity of the relationship and the basic *shape* of the Arena to interpersonal climates and, therefore, to the *quality* of the relationship. So, the graphic displays of one's scores helps to pinpoint both the size and shape effects his behaviors are having. In addition to the effects of status differences on one's predispositions which the test addresses, it becomes possible to talk about "personality types" which would use or fail to use excessively the basic processes. All in all, it makes for a quite stimulating and soul-searching session.*

---

*From personal correspondence of Jay Hall. Reprinted by permission.

Anita Simon and Yvonne Agazarian use the Johari model in their study, *Sequential Analysis of Verbal Interaction* (SAVI). They sys-

Communication Model from Two Points of View: Teacher and Class*

	Information Unknown To Class	Information Known To Class
Information Known to Teacher	Secret Area	Public Area
Information Unknown to Teacher	Unknown Area	Blind Area

Drawing A
Communication Model with Teacher as "Self"

	Information Unknown To Teacher	Information Known To Teacher
Information Known to Class	Secret Area	Public Area
Information Unknown to Class	Unknown Area	Blind Area

Drawing B
Communication Model with Class as "Self"

---

*From *Sequential Analysis of Verbal Interaction* by Anita Simon and Yvonne Agazarian, page 95. Copyright October, 1967 by Anita Simon and Yvonne Agazarian. Reprinted by permission.

tematically develop instruments and techniques for the study of inter-action, particularly in the classroom, and they use the Johari Window as their communication model to show how "real and potential information" may be operationally described.

The authors use this version of the model to represent the flow of communication for a teacher returning unsatisfactory test papers. They show how the data is gathered and analyzed and how the results may be used to improve classroom interaction. As in Professor Hall's studies, mentioned earlier, these data can be made available to the participants, and, with the aid of the Johari awareness model, the information can be clearly presented in a relatively nonjudgmental fashion. The authors point out that data collected and fed back in this way is invariably useful in stimulating persons to examine and to learn about their relationships with others. Apparently, the approach is fresh enough and sufficiently free of loaded terms to enable a flow of information and additional interaction.

Interaction and Influence

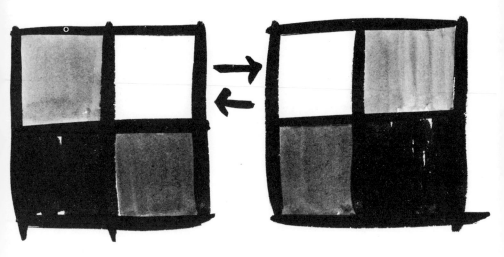

Leadership: The Leader as a Shaman

What is leadership? Are there different kinds of leadership?

For the word "leader," use teacher, consultant, boss, healer, trainer, counselor, therapist, executive, director, or chairman. Whoever takes responsibility for influencing others through interpersonal behavior may be understood as a leader.

The anthropologist Merrill Jackson (as reported by Adelson, 1961) proposes an intriguing set of models gleaned from different cultures. For speculative purposes, these models may be viewed as a fivefold typology. Each of us, then, fits one of the leader types, whether we are aware of it or not. Of course, perfect fit is only hypothetical, but nevertheless we may see ourselves as resembling one type more closely than another. The five types are shaman, mystic, naturalist, priest, and magician. In the following descriptions, each type is viewed with the aid of the Johari Window.

The shaman deals with others and with subject matter to call attention to himself and to enhance himself. He uses personal power to influence or to heal; he employs craft, charm, and cunning. He knows

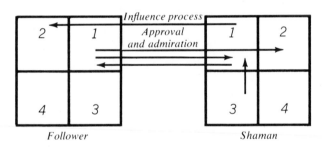

Follower   Shaman

how you will respond to certain of his actions; he will reveal bits of information in such a way as to impress upon you how able and admirable he is. He will demonstrate his power so that you will be pleased and come to rely on him and to be impressed by him. You will come away feeling better and you will think he is wonderful. You will trust him and come to believe nearly everything he tells you because he has shown his craft and skill and he has done so with confidence in himself and with satisfaction in your attention to him.

In Johari terms, the shaman calls attention to himself by what he skillfully reveals, Q3 to Q1. He pays attention to step-by-step disclosure, noting the effect on you. He genuinely enjoys being admired so that as you view him in Q1 and Q2 the shaman feels rewarded. All four quadrants of the shaman are excited by the attention you pay him. He may thus become more confident, more dramatic, and more spontaneous. And the learner or subordinate or client may become more enthralled. The person so influenced may learn a lot and be quite excited about what he is experiencing, but not without hazards. Dependency may create problems for the learner both in the subject matter learned and in the relationships formed. Because the shaman is more narcissistic than other leaders, he may mislead the follower about the relationship expected by the follower. Further, the follower may feel let down in trying to transfer his learning to another interpersonal situation and find that without the charisma of the shaman the results are disappointing.

The shaman may fail with followers who have their own narcissistic problems. Their need to call attention to themselves may conflict with the shaman so that charisma never develops and a distaste instead may ensue.

The influence of the shaman-type leader is highly variable. Frequently the impression he makes is strong but temporary, like the effect of a successful performer. He may influence observers to muse about rising to the shaman's spectacular heights, but when the show is over, the others return to their mundane lives and limited aspirations.

The leader as shaman may appear modest and humble; he is not always the exhibitionist. No matter, the attention is always focused on him. He will in quiet or flamboyant ways call attention to his own personality in dealing with the subject matter. Unusual ability transforms the shaman into the charismatic leader, and then the effect of vivacity, originality, and forcefulness may be spectacular.

Yet there is something about the self-centered display that may repel some and place others on guard. Perhaps, as Adelson states (1961, p. 396), it depends on the particular form of narcissism. Is the implicit message, "Admire me, love me," or is it the more vindictive, "I'm great, but I don't know about you. I don't need you"? The shaman as narcissistic teacher, the platform personality, attracts a large following, but he may also be despised by many. Regardless of his favorable or unfavorable impact, the anxiety filtering through the shaman's style affects his followers and cautions against the temptation to regress.

In Johari terms, the shaman's first quadrant becomes suffused with behavior and feelings of his second and fourth quadrants. The latter are unavailable to him directly because they are areas of unresolved behavior tinged with anxiety and with childlike qualities. This excitement heightens his performance, but may threaten some of his followers.

The Leader as a Mystic

The mystic leads, teaches, or heals by seeking out hidden sources of weakness and of strength in his followers. He is unusually sensitive and perceptive and works hard at uncovering the unique qualities of his followers. He devotes his energy and attention to divining hidden

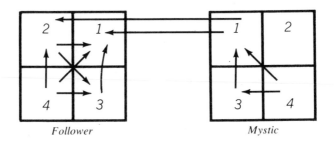

Follower   Mystic

flaws, and he is skillful in figuring out the underlying causes of difficulties. The true mystic works in the same light as others but he sees and feels more and thus appears to have extraordinary vision. He is genuinely altruistic, giving of himself in a special and personal way to all. He searches out idiosyncrasies and dwells on the special attributes of those who follow him. He is versatile and flexible in approach; he can relate to each person in a way which reflects the uniqueness of the other. His followers come away enriched or strengthened and with a feeling of confidence in this type of leader.

However, the mystic is a difficult model to imitate because of the unusual gifts required. Even if one were sufficiently sensitive, perceptive, and skillful in working with others, this would not be enough. Genuine altruism is rare, demanding selflessness without ambivalence. It means holding aside one's own needs and interests while working with others. It comes from a genuine effort to work with a particular person or group so that growth, achievement, and learning can take place *without incurring psychological indebtedness*. This type of leader is indeed a rare individual. He does not seek dependency from individuals; quite the contrary. Nor does he seek a large following, for his altruism is not a disguised need for power or popularity.

At best, imitations of the mystic appear mechanical and never quite come off; at worst they are a form of expediency. Trying to appear altruistic when one is not is bound to backfire and result in bitter feelings and lowered achievement.

The Leader as a Naturalist

As a leader, consultant, teacher, or healer, the naturalist is essentially realistic, factual, and impersonal. He wants to find out what the problem is and to go to work on it directly. He is not interested in the personality of his followers, his subordinates, his students, or his clients. There's a job to be done and the best thing to do is get on with it. Feelings are simply not important to the naturalist-leader and an undue display of emotion is frowned upon. Reason is the mode; facts count. Empirically tested methods are recommended. Wherever possible information acquired by means of scientifically oriented methods ology has highest priority. His own personality is kept out of the picture to the point where he may be criticized for being cold and impersonal. Modern physicians going about their busy rounds or dealing with an office full of patients are sometimes seen this way. Patients complain that they are inspected, tapped, poked, and moved about as if they were cattle or pieces of complicated machinery. But the naturalist in whatever position is respected for his results, and for him that's what counts. He does not mean to offend anyone, its just that his style of working leaves little room for personal idiosyncrasy. He is cool and skillful even though at home he may be relaxed, warm, and quite demonstrative with his family. As a teacher, he is usually very well organized. His lectures are clear and precise but on the colorless side. He assumes his students are sufficiently motivated and well organized not to need any special techniques to help them learn. The notes students take read like a textbook, which is what they are intended to be.

The naturalist-leader working in a group where emotional matters are more important than cognitive ones behaves in a recognizable manner. He has a well-planned design with clear stipulations for each stage of work. Objectives are made explicit at every step; didactic explanations are frequent and formal lectures are important. The lectures are filled with facts, information, and theories, and copious reading material is assigned. Participants have the right at any time to bring up questions and to demand explanations. It is not surprising therefore that emotional crises are rather infrequent; they are not permitted to get out of hand. Intuitive interventions are infrequent. Skill exercises of all kinds are carefully prepared and executed. Large problems are broken down into smaller ones and taken one at a time. Authoritative sources are relied on to assure tried and tested approaches in exercises

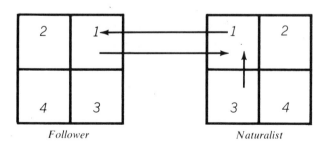

Follower   Naturalist

and lectures. In the group, the naturalist leader may reveal his feelings when they are particularly relevant and clear. He never loses control of the group or of himself even if his manner is soft and easygoing. Information moves from Q3 to Q1 of the naturalist-leader. He is interested in direct communication, and he stays in the first quadrant as much as possible. The third quadrant is his storehouse of knowledge and skill to be drawn on as necessary. On the job, he is task oriented; in a group he is not interested in the participants' second quadrants except as they may bear on a particular problem. The nature of the leader-follower relationship is clear and explicit; contractual obligations and objectives are spelled out wherever possible.

The Leader as a Priest

As an anthropologist, Merrill Jackson sees the priest as a particular kind of healer. The priest is effective because he represents an omnipotent authority; he claims no special personal power. Joseph Adelson (1961, p. 397) sees a parallel in "the teacher who stresses not his personal virtues, but his membership in a powerful or admirable collectivity, for example, physics, psychoanalysis, classical scholarship." Recognizing that institutions and organizations differ widely in their formality, structure, and openness, he nevertheless can identify priestly modes of behavior. He notes how this teacher model influences students by invoking certain institutional characteristics. In a similar fashion a leader or consultant or trainer might be seen as taking on the priestly role when he emphasizes the following (Adelson, 1961, pp. 397-8):

1. Continuity: the past, present, and future of the organization guide the leader's daily work.

2. Hierarchy: the leader or trainer derives his authority from a par-

ticular status in relation to the power structure. He uses certain great names who hold an exalted place in the institution. The followers (or participants) are also expected to revere these great people and to look forward to the time when they can take their places in the hierarchy.

3. Election: since membership is a way of achieving immediate power, the leader or trainer rewards his disciple by approving him for selection. But first the novice must be trained and disciplined to endure the trials and tests of initiation. Self-transformation is expected before the privileges of membership are granted.

4. Mission: the organization frequently offers a program for some important change or reform, and the leader or trainer espouses his utopian view with missionary zeal. The follower or trainee is expected to absorb this zeal and to influence others in the same way.

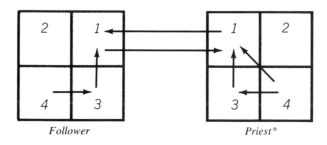

Follower   Priest*

In the priestly model, the leader, consultant, or trainer works closely with his follower, instructing him explicitly, but frequently implicitly, in all aspects of his life. The camaraderie of association with others going through the process helps the recruit through the more difficult times when fatigue, depression, and doubts set in. The air of confidence and, indeed, of certainty surrounding the institution and the leaders helps enormously at such times. Minor intraorganizational differences disappear when under attack; the novice is not admitted to the deeper internal frictions until he is well along the hierarchical ladder himself.

---

*Here, Q4 refers to religious feelings that bear on the interaction, when these are present. Otherwise, the focus of action is apt to be Q3 to Q1 for the priest and Q1 for the follower.

The Leader as a Magician

Except for a brief description, Adelson does not enlarge on the magician's way of working and healing. I have taken the liberty of expanding the magician's role following Merrill Jackson's definition as quoted by Adelson: "The magician heals through his knowledge of arcane and complex rules, and his ability to follow ritual precisely" (p. 394). He has secret knowledge like the ancient alchemist who could turn base metals into gold. Only he has the special knowledge and skill to create an elixir with which he heals the sick and dying. He may not agree to work on every problem, but once he embarks upon a search for a solution, he does not fail.

The magician sets up his own work conditions with which no one must interfere. He may call upon others to bring him special supplies and equipment, though he never explains just what these things will do. He will be highly critical of the materials for unexplained reasons until they meet his secret standards. The simplest things are included in his equipment; but some of the materials are entirely of his own making and no one else can duplicate them. He will start and end according to certain signs for reasons known only to him. As he goes about his work he appears to be guided by hidden cues, totally absorbed in ritual. At times, he seems oblivious to his surroundings and no one may disturb him. He gives the appearance of being driven in his work by forces which he alone can perceive. He may give greatly of himself to the point that he suffers as if in some kind of ordeal.

Purity of spirit, perfection in ritual, total concentration on the magical incantation are all-important. Nothing else matters. The magician appears to be guided by mysterious natural and supernatural phenomena; he is in touch with the essence of things. He cares nothing for his appearance or well-being provided the ritual is carried out exactly as it should. He holds himself responsible for the task he has undertaken; there is no turning back. Once he sets into motion a series of events with his followers and with the sick one who needs healing, no one must interfere with the flow of things. There is a hidden logic and intelligence at work which informs and guides his conduct, but he never explains. He is contemptuous of rational approaches; he ignores his critics and detractors. He is guided by a different order of things and as long as he follows this secret procedure his magic will have power to influence and to heal with incredible success.

The magician interacts with his followers in special and limited ways. The follower places himself in the hands of the magician from the start. He trusts the magician implicitly and makes little effort to fathom

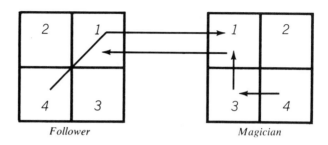

Follower   Magician

his ways. The follower is more passive and dependent during the ritual. It is not that he relates to the magician so much as he relies on his magic. He does try to please the magician so that the solutions come faster and the healing effects are more powerful. The magician alone knows when and where the follower holds himself back. The magician suffers anguish privately when this occurs, though he may complain to his followers that he cannot work without their wholehearted support. He thereby carries the relevant community with him and he can tell by mysterious signs when all is going well. The followers know that the magician type of leader is a loner. The followers fit into his scheme of things or not at all. Generally, they leave him alone but try to stay on good terms by gifts and praise of special kinds. He is called upon at times of crisis, leaving more mundane matters to others.

What Kind of a Leader Are You?

A summary of the five models in terms of key qualities is shown in the chart below. Although each kind of healer (leader, consultant, teacher, trainer, etc.) interacts with his followers in terms of all four quadrants, the unique styles are best understood by abstracting the main focus of interaction.

	Leader	*Follower*
Shaman	Q1, Q2, Q3	Q1, Q2
Mystic	Q1, Q4	Q1, Q2, Q3, Q4
Naturalist	Q1, Q3	Q1
Priest	Q1, Q3, Q4	Q1, Q3, Q4
Magician	Q3, Q4	Q1, Q2

What good are these leadership models? We don't have mystics, shamans, magicians, or priests in our outfit. We run a school or a business or an institution.

True; however, these models cut across cultural boundaries and suggest certain universal ways in which people influence each other. We know that great diversity exists in our own culture to the point that no single model of leadership and of relationships is adequate.

Extending these healer models to college teaching as Adelson has done is enlightening. Going further into other leadership situations is worth a try. In industry the realistic, task-oriented naturalist type would appear to be the right one. But just about every organization or institution complains about communication problems and leadership hangups. And every other outfit talks uneasily about morale, especially at the lower levels of the organization.

If the physician is too much the naturalist with the patient, then the nurse, the technician, and the social worker take over more of the healing process.

A capable physician at a conference on "Working with the Handicapped" complained about patients who for some strange reasons never returned for their prosthetic devices even when costs were covered by outside sources. It was difficult for others at the conference, including handicapped persons, to describe to the physician the need for each patient to be seen and dealt with as an individual. To be treated as a whole person was an important process in the healing function even if only part of the patient required medical attention.

Employees in industry are just like patients in many respects, and graduate students are really not much different, either. They are individuals in complex settings working under authorities or experts, trying to accomplish something, influencing others and being influenced, in a system of rewards which are only partially internalized by the followers. Leaders or healers are themselves products of such situations and carry with them modes of response which reflect their earlier experiences. Early family relations are of course basic to the way one follows and leads.

In encounter groups or human relations training labs, the leader or trainer can often be understood in terms of the model he most closely represents. Is he priestly, acting merely as an agent for some powerful authority? Does he show great personal force, charming the participants and in turn being charmed by their adulation, like a shaman? Does he concentrate in a sensitive and intuitive way on each person, searching out the uniqueness in the individual and the group interaction, as a mystic would? Is he engrossed in a hidden design, pursuing his objectives by unraveling a magic ritual which he alone seems to comprehend? Is he straightforward and objective even when the most personal issues are involved, preferring an empirical, naturalistic approach and clearly set goals.

I think it is a mistake to expect all leaders or trainers to follow one model. We can demand that they do a competent job in an ethical manner, but the style and mode must be left to each one of them. *Each of the models has strengths and weaknesses.* The trap facing the naturalist is different from that facing the shaman, as mentioned above. The shaman may need help in understanding the effects of his narcissism; the naturalist may need to realize what his impersonal approach does to people. The trainer as magician might be just as effective if he were not quite so secretive or ritualistic. The leader who is priestly influences others to work and to learn, but he can set into motion an authoritarian chain effect which could interfere with growth. Does the leader functioning as a mystic realize the difference between genuine and expedient altruism? Does he have such great inner strength and resources that he can give of himself unstintingly without asking anything in return? Can he know that the touch of sour vindictiveness he occasionally experiences is a chronic hazard to one who sets high altruistic standards?

In brief, every leader or trainer:

functions according to some basic healer model.

emphasizes certain quadrants of the Johari model in his interactions.

has strengths and weaknesses intrinsic to his basic model.

follows inherently a different goal according to the basic healer model he represents.

uses a particular set of means-ends processes.

Having set down in rather exaggerated fashion what leadership means in terms of the five anthropological models, I should like to comment on some difficulties with reality. The models are fine, but the problem is with the real leaders or trainers or consultants or therapists or teachers who do not fit the models. My interest is in offering a wider lens through which to view the influence process rather than in presenting another leadership typology. The healer models are particularly useful because they invoke the hidden, secret, and unknown quadrants of human behavior in comprehensible guises. The models do not exhaust the range of human perception and interaction, but they do cover a lot of territory which has been excluded from most contemporary discussion in and out of academic institutions. Mixed models must exist; let's try a few. The charismatic naturalist? The priestly leader whose rituals are carried out on the job with the magician's secret ways? The sensitive and altruistic mystic who writes clear, objective textbooks for his trade? The models cannot be mixed at random because certain qualities are incompatible. The richness of actual human personality does offer more variety than exists in any set of models. But the value of these leadership guides is to help in grasping a central dominant quality of a particular leader. Then, as necessary, one can qualify the most pertinent model with characteristics of other models, though one should not lose sight of the main model qualities. (It occurs to me as I write this that my mystic bias is revealed when I urge applying the models to help get at the essence of the individual leader, but selecting a scheme that covers a broad range of styles based on empirical anthropological evidence probably shows that I have a naturalistic allegiance too.)

The five models vary with reference to need for structure. It is clear that the priest and naturalist need and use more structure, whether working alone or within an organization, the shaman and mystic less structure, and the magician somewhere in the middle. The structure for the magician type does not come from others or from an organization but from some secret and mysterious source to which he alone has access.

One View of a Typical Industrial Organization

The statement below may be thought of as a single-item test. Read it and then mark the choice beneath it that most closely represents your reaction.

There are many kinds of personal relations which exist in a typical industrial organization where people are merely going on living their daily lives with no crises or shocks or bewildering complications to try them. Yet every individual in the organization is clinging to his individual identity, is in fear of losing it in the general organizational flavor. As in most organizations, the mere struggle to have anything of one's own, to be oneself at all, creates an element of strain which keeps everybody almost at the breaking point. One realizes that even in harmonious organizations there is this double life: the public life which is the one we can observe in another person's organization, and underneath another — secret and intense — which is the real life that stamps the faces and gives character to the voices of our friends. Always in his mind each member of these social units is escaping, running away, trying to break the net which circumstance and his own feelings have woven about him. One realizes that human relationships are the tragic necessity of human life; that they can never be wholly satisfactory, that every ego is half the time greedily seeking them and half the time pulling away from them. In those simple relationships of colleagues, supervisors and those supervised, experts, technicians and administrators, men of action and men of ideas, there are innumerable shades of satisfaction and anxiety which make up the patterns of our lives day by day.

What is your reaction to this statement? Check the response that comes closest to your own:

    ☐ I agree   ☐ I disagree
    ☐ I agree strongly   ☐ I disagree strongly

Before discussing the statement further, I should say that it was originally about family life and that it has been adapted to apply to institutions. For example, the last sentence of the original reads, "In those simple relationships of loving husband and wife, affectionate sisters, children and grandmother, there are innumerable shades of sweetness and anguish which make up the patterns of our lives day by day." The author is Willa Cather (*Not Under Forty*, 1936, New York: Knopf) and the original passage is quoted by Charlotte Towle (1952, p. 81) to shed light on family relations.

I have given the adapted statement to industrial managers, technical workers, and scientists who work in large organizations. I've also collected reactions from nurses and nurse administrators, and from professional and technical staff members of mental hospitals on the same statement, modified only to apply to the respondents' job titles. The results are similar to those obtained with college students:

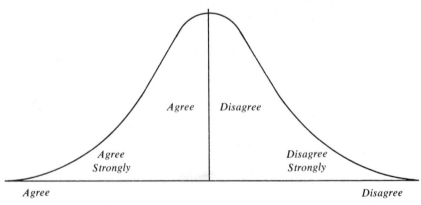

As I have noted, this is a single-item test which reveals something of the complexity of people and of organizations. The test item has been variously modified to fit the situations of the people tested. Yet the reactions distribute themselves, if the sample is large enough, into a neat, normal-type curve. Respondents split about half and half on agree-disagree, with far fewer at the extreme positions than at the moderate positions.

After collecting these reactions and summarizing them in a group, I initiate an open discussion. At first there is consternation that others see relationships so differently; people consider it incredible that they are talking about the same organization or the same statement. After a while, participants on both sides attack the language in the statement, implying thereby that the discrepancy is not that big. But the fact remains that huge differences exist. We do live in very different worlds, affective and cognitive. We vary tremendously in accessibility to feelings from within and to events around us. As we try to communicate with each other, we face the same differences in feeling and thinking and experiencing. It may be true enough for you and me that in our organizations "the mere struggle to have anything of one's own, to be oneself at all, creates an element of strain which keeps everybody almost at the breaking point." But suppose that for one of us this is a Q3 phenomenon—known to you but hidden from others. And for the other one of us it is a Q2 experience which others can observe but to which the person himself is blind. Now try to communicate. Try, for example, to face a crisis that comes up in the organization. Or for that matter, try making a significant change in the organization. Now the fat sizzles. How and where do you start? How long will it take before an exchange can take place that bears on organizational events and people's lives? Sad to say, most of us will not even attempt to deal with what is involved in the situation. Note, I am not addressing myself to healing or helping people personally, only to concern with what is actually going on in this organization with these people. When we add power differentials to the already complicated relationships, then indeed do we have a no-man's land seeded with mines and booby traps.

If this picture has any validity, then we are all in a hell of a mess, and we can expect perennial and often unpredicted explosions—in the company, the school, the committee, the neighborhood, the family, the professional organization. What looks like a going concern is frequently an uneasy moratorium among persons who feel no one understands them. They even forget sometimes that the working guise, the job role, is not the same as the person. In a brief weekend conference recently, after a rather frank and thorough exploration of some facets of one man's work life, an able and perceptive colleague exclaimed, "Four years and forty feet down the hall—and I never knew you, never knew you at all." This, mind you, was in a small unit where people collaborated daily in their work and seemed to know each other quite well.

☐ *"Day by day, hour by hour, we misunderstand each other because we cross well-marked boundaries; we blur the sense of you out there and me here; we merge, frequently very sloppily, the subjective with the objective, in various ways. We make of the other person simply an extension of self, either through the attribution of our own thoughts and attitudes to the other person, or by too facile a decision about his nature, after which we go on responding to him as though he were the character we invented. Or we force him-her into the role of surrogate for some member of the original cast."*—Hiram Haydn (1965, pp. 25-26)

The way we differ, one from another, would be a serious enough problem even if we each had equivalent awareness of ourself and others. We could perhaps differ in values, ideology, and interests but have roughly the same awareness of feelings and behavior. But to have different values and ideology *and* vastly different awareness of what is going on in us and around us—well, I think that's just about where we stand. It suggests that the way out of no-man's land via the communication process is just as precarious as the mine field itself. The prospects would not be so gloomy if it were possible to change some of the priorities implicit in the way we work, go to school, teach, raise a family, conduct a business, or run a hospital. By that I mean that the time may have arrived when the concern for people's understanding of each other and of themselves may demand as much time as the work itself does. In the long run this may mean greater production and less destruction. But even if there were no guarantees of greater efficiency, which is hard to believe, there would still be a case for more time and attention to these softer matters. Coming to a better understanding of self and others is a slow, painstaking process, though it has its own satisfaction and excitement. The task moves slowly because each of us apparently operates out of a different set of assumptions. We may make the revolutionary discovery of how we are each blind about things others see. And we may learn how to tell when it's all right to disclose what we have hidden from others. We may come to learn that by allowing differences to be expressed it really is possible to enlarge our own awareness. We may discover that though it can be painful to learn new things about self and others, it is far more painful and costly not to learn. We may find out about the special class of satisfactions which can only come from releasing more of ourselves to be ourselves. And we may savor the relief that comes from fewer battles and stalemates going on between us and inside each of us.

Since power and influence are such significant and often insidious issues it is to be expected that in learning about real people working in a real organization we will uncover parts of the power network. There may be clarification of real versus imagined power, of formal versus informal power, and of designated versus self-appropriated influence. It would be enlightening indeed for employees at any level to get to know something of the pressures to which colleagues and fellow employees are exclusively subjected.

I have in mind a manager who felt he had to take orders from a highly placed political figure. Since this was a quasipublic organization, the manager had very little choice. He could either carry out the order quietly and violate one of the organization's rules, or resist the order and face the consequences. In an organizational learning lab, associates of this manager were surprised to learn about this source of pressure and became quite sympathetic to the long-suffering manager. Now instead of just griping at the violation of rules they collaborated to help him and the organization deal with the realities of impinging power.

Feedback

Sending signals to find out where you are and what you are getting into has been characteristic of animals, and particularly of man, long before cybernetics gave us the term for it. Feedback is not a pleasant sounding word, but it is difficult to find another one as clear and useful. In its simplest sense, feedback refers to the return to you of behavior you have generated.

☐ *"The turning back of the experience of the individual upon himself... is the essential condition, within the social process, for the development of mind." —* Buckley (1967, p. 100)

That morning look at the mirror before shaving is a kind of feedback. The mirror speaks loud and clear, but it doesn't have much of a memory. A camera does, and for this reason it can be a bit more threatening. Videotape playback has become an important means for teaching and learning about behavior, and it has enlarged on the function of the tape recorder for this purpose. But the most powerful form of feedback is the human response. People can be excellent mirrors, cameras, and tape recorders. Optimal learning, however, requires sensitivity and judgment in the feedback process, and for this reason human response remains the most powerful instrument. Teaching machines are ingenious devices performing all kinds of feedback functions; but they have a long way to go in registering, reacting to, and reporting back on the qualities of human behavior. Man-machine interaction is limited to the information stored in the machine by the programmer. The machine does not have second and fourth quadrants. It is conceivable that the

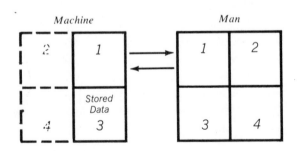

machine could be wired to the man so that physiological changes concomitant with emotional states might be registered. Blood pressure, electroencephalograms and psychogalvanic changes in skin conductivity (sweating), for example, could be recorded and entered into the storage chambers (Q3) of the machine and then fed back through its open quadrant to the person. The meaning of these physiological changes would, however, remain ambiguous. Differentiating anxiety from irritation, anger from assertiveness, and pleasure from tension, for example, would be difficult if not impossible. Ambivalence and volatility of feelings and their referents would pose tough problems, to say the least. In addition, physiological states have duration and lag-time factors, thereby compounding the difficulties for the electronic instruments.

Man in a feedback role has problems too. He is always faced with a choice of behavior from which to extract pertinent messages. As Laing (1961) and Gibb (1961) emphasize, even the simplest communication may be misinterpreted and misunderstood. The same may be said for every silence. Nevertheless, it is hypothetically possible to map out relatively simplified feedback patterns.

Varieties of Feedback

Since even the simplest exchange may be misunderstood and thus quickly escalate interactional difficulties, it is useful to be able to check with the other person when necessary. The manner is direct but relatively unobtrusive. It should be obvious that even this simple matter can be transformed into a challenge or an attack as in, "Did you say 'good' morning?" Or, try repeating "good morning" through clenched teeth, just to feel the effect. Five varieties of feedback may be distinguished and illustrated with the aid of the Johari awareness model.

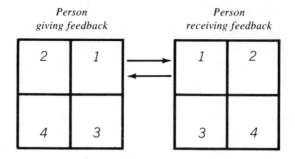

Person
giving feedback

Person
receiving feedback

1. Information. The person giving feedback (G) repeats to the person receiving feedback (R) what the latter said. For instance, "Did you say that he did not speak for you?" This variety of feedback often is prefaced with remarks such as "if I heard you right" or "did you mean to say that," or "am I correct in saying." These prefatory remarks let the receiver of feedback, R, know that the content of the communication itself is being checked. When R hears the verbatim feedback he has a chance to modify or to confirm the essentials of his message.

2. Personal reaction. The person giving feedback (G) informs R of the effect he is having on G. Since the person receiving feedback usually is not aware of G's reaction, G discloses this from his third quadrant. For example, G states, "When you said that I felt very uncomfortable." Or, "I've been annoyed with you all morning, but since you came to Dale's defense I feel differently toward you."

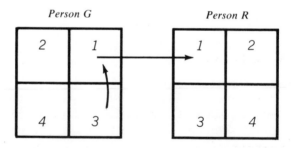

Person G

Person R

The personal reaction feedback is one of the most significant learning events in group interaction. In effect, the individual is informed of a specific impact on another person. All too frequently such reactions are censored in everyday exchanges. The reasons offered for censoring are themselves revealing, such as not wanting to "hurt someone's feelings," or "that's the way you lose friends" or "why rock the boat," or "I'll bide my time before I let him have it." Censorship takes the form of politeness, silence, displaced reaction (feedback to the wrong person) or aborted interaction, among other forms.

3. _Judgmental reaction._ The person giving feedback evaluates the behavior of the other and delivers an opinion. For example, G says, "Why do you stick with this job? Anyone can tell you're a better engineer than you are a supervisor." Or, "You have no business jumping on Ed here just because he keeps quiet."

Person G				Person R	
2	1		1	2	
4	3		3	4	

In the first example, G gives R advice, presumably for the latter's own good. This kind of feedback is familiar and can be found almost anywhere. Judgmental reactions tend to be resisted and may even fix the position of the receiver more firmly. The different opinions are apt to be argued pro and con. Even when judgments _are_ solicited there is little effect since the individual is often seeking a particular opinion. When a group has worked to a high level of trust such reactions may still be made by members but the reception is somewhat different. Opinions then carry more weight though they may still be resisted. At times, thoughtful evaluations serve to open new areas to be examined by G, R, and others in the group. In general, though judgmental reactions seem inevitable, they are among the least desirable kinds of feedback for influencing awareness and change.

4. Forced feedback. The person giving feedback calls attention to behavior in the other's blind area: "Can't you see you've deliberately attacked everyone who has taken a position of leadership?"

The assumption here is that R was not aware of his own feelings, and this may have been true. G may even confront R with behavioral evi-

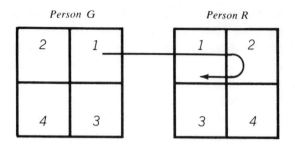

Person G   Person R

dence such as *R*'s tense expression, the change in voice tone, etc. Such unsolicited feedback may be undesirable depending on the relationship between the two, the group climate, the insight potential of *R*, and the antecedent events. More important, the outcome depends on what is going on in *R* and in the relationship, and why he was not in touch with his own affect. Leaders, teachers, therapists, and others who work with people differ markedly on this feedback dimension. The bias of this writer is to work toward group conditions in which participants make their own discoveries and disclosures. In particular, the leader's use of such feedback tends to carry much force and generally should be avoided. There are many ways of facilitating introspection as needed, but the important matters are the stage of development of the group, the nature of the ongoing relationships, and the resources of the particular individual receiving feedback.

5. Interpretation. A variant of forced feedback, interpretation means explaining conduct by relating behavior to a reason or motive. For

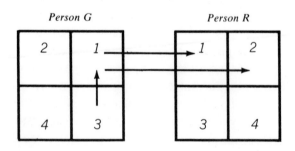

Person G   Person R

example, *G* might say, "Maybe you feel low because this is our last meeting." In this instance, *R* may reveal, Q3 to Q1, that he is depressed

G believes he has an insight into the reason of which *R* is unaware (Q2) and which *G* expresses.

Interpretation is obviously a complex and subtle kind of feedback, one that is best used sparsely if at all. The timing and phrasing are highly important. When is the individual ready to see and to understand his own motive, his own trauma and conflict? What strengths and weaknesses does he have? What related problems tie into this one of which the interpreter is unaware? How much time is available to deal with the new anxieties released? To what extent is the receiver feeling cornered and panicky with these loaded disclosures? Will such interpretations increase dependency and arouse other kinds of transference problems? The list of cautions can be extended and perhaps overextended. We are well within the realm of psychotherapy in this form of feedback, especially where the earlier history of the individual is involved and where highly charged conflicts and trauma lie deep in the second and fourth quadrants. Schools of psychotherapy differ strongly on this issue (see Ford and Urban, 1963). And above all, the research concerning the effectiveness of interpretations for learning and growth is still inconclusive (Colby, 1964). Behavior in interaction is so rich and meaningful in its own right that references to remote and indirect explanations are rarely necessary. The ahistorical Lewinian thesis (1947) makes good sense: what is significant in the individual's past exists in his present attitudes and behavior. The ingredients for learning and growth, therefore, also exist in the present. It may well be true that "he who can not recall his past is doomed to repeat it." However, it may be even more true that he who does not comprehend his present ways will never understand his past.

Jack Gibb, writing on "Defensive Communication" (1961), makes a valuable analysis of feedback problems. Gibb focuses attention on the interpersonal climate as crucial in determining how a particular communication will be interpreted:

In working over an eight-year period with recordings of discussions occurring in varied settings, the writer developed the six pairs of defensive and supportive categories presented in Table 1. Behavior which a listener perceives as possessing any of the characteristics listed in the left-hand column arouses defensiveness, whereas that which he interprets as having any of the qualities designated as supportive reduces defensive feelings. The degree to which these reactions occur depends upon the personal level of defensiveness and upon the general climate in the group at the time.

Speech or other behavior which appears evaluative increases defensiveness. If by expression, manner of speech, tone of voice, or verbal content the sender seems to be evaluating or judging the listener, then the receiver goes on guard. Of course, other factors may inhibit the reaction. If the listener thought that the speaker regarded him as an equal and was being open and spontaneous, for example, the evaluativeness in a message would be neutralized and perhaps not even perceived. This same principle applies equally to the other five categories of potentially defense-producing climates. The six sets are interactive.

TABLE I

Categories of Behavior Characteristic of Supportive
and Defensive Climates in Small Groups

Defensive Climates	Supportive Climates
1. Evaluation	1. Description
2. Control	2. Problem orientation
3. Strategy	3. Spontaneity
4. Neutrality	4. Empathy
5. Superiority	5. Equality
6. Certainty	6. Provisionalism

Because our attitudes toward other persons are frequently, and often necessarily, evaluative, expressions which the defensive person will regard as nonjudgmental are hard to frame. Even the simplest question usually conveys the answer that the sender wishes or implies the response that would fit into his value system. A mother, for example, immediately following an earth tremor that shook the house, sought for her small son with the question: "Bobby, where are you?" The timid and plaintive "Mommy, I didn't do it" indicated how Bobby's chronic mild defensiveness predisposed him to react with a projection of his own guilt and in the context of his chronic assumption that questions are full of accusation.*

*From "Defensive Communication" by Jack R. Gibb in *The Journal of Communication*, vol. 11, no. 3, September, 1961, pp. 142-43, published by The National Society for the Study of Communication. Reprinted by permission.

Heuristic

What do you know about yourself now that you did not know five years ago? Have you changed? If so, how? In what way will you change in the next five years? What understanding will you have that you do not now have?

Somehow you have changed. More experience, different experience, and new conditions have affected you — in addition to your growing five years older. It is nevertheless difficult to identify what you have learned on your job or in school or at home that makes for this difference. What you have gained by experience is not always translatable into language. In fact, it rarely is.

I spoke earlier of Q2 and Q4 as areas of which you lack awareness yet which are the sources of new understanding. Behavior and experience in these quadrants ripen, like fruit on a tree, and may in time be harvested provided conditions are favorable. Experience may lead to ideas, information, and insight. Ideas, information, and insight may lead to new experience and new feelings. There is two-way traffic. Becoming aware of the way you work with others is remarkably complex. No one will tell you. Or you will be told just a part of how you behave.

"You never talk to me directly," one colleague might say.

"You smile all the time. It confuses me."

"You're a different guy in the meetings. Your voice sounds deeper but more hollow. It just sounds a little phony."

Information such as this may indeed affect the way you feel and may affect your immediate experience. It is difficult to know what kinds of situations increase the traffic between ideas and experience. In many work and school situations, such exchanges might paralyze traffic and impede understanding. Under optimal conditions, where concern for persons at least matches concern for work, the process of transforming experience into awareness and awareness into new experience can take place.

"I wasn't aware that I never speak directly to you. But even now as I'm doing just that I realize I feel very uneasy. Come to think of it, I've always assumed that you were a direct pipeline up to the front office." The speaker was on his way to understanding a bit more about the dog-eat-dog atmosphere at the office as he perceived it. But the competition was partly his own view of things. Others who were not as ambitious and hard driving saw much collaboration with the other departments and with the front office along with some competition. There was concern for people in the organization, but the speaker was preoccupied with his own progress and the competition standing in his way.

In short, learning about how you get along with others and learning about how you get along with yourself occur simultaneously. Your learning about experience and experiencing new learning occur reciprocally and usually simultaneously.

Interaction Values

Trust and Appropriate Self-Disclosure

Some self-disclosure, Q3 to Q1, is essential before new learning about the blind area, Q2, can begin. Why then are universal trust and universal self-disclosure not advocated?

Warnings come from all quarters, from *caveat emptor*, let the buyer beware, to *cave canem*, beware the dog, and these admonitions have come up through the history of human experience. Our coins tell us, "In God we trust." On matters of life and death we trust our physicians, politicians, airline pilots. We have little choice. Advertisers implore us to trust their products. Attractive people on television tell us in effect to trust them and not our own sense data.

The real issue is trust in human relationships, and here everyone runs scared. People are afraid of people at least as much as people need people; perhaps it is because people need people that they are afraid. In most new groups there is a mixture of excitement and anxiety. In new social groups, new classes, new encounter groups, or new business contacts, the most predictable reaction is a rise in tension. A clear illustration of the meaning of interpersonal tension is the mother who discovers that the days when company drops in is the time when her infant is most apt to throw up his food. The child is breast fed and apparently responds to both the physiological and psychological changes in the mother and in the rest of her household. In one experiment (Luft, 1966, reprinted as Appendix 2 in this book), two students who did not know each other were asked to sit across a room from each other in silence and to note their reactions on a piece of paper. Initially, the most conspicuous feeling was tension or anxiety. This was reported in private interviews with each subject (*S*) after each experiment. Later, even without words, the subjects "came to terms" with each other and were more comfortable. When a stranger was introduced to this dyad, again anxiety rose and negative feelings were expressed by the *S's* toward the stranger on the rating sheets. There was no customary or conventional set for occasions such as this experimental one, and the *S's* had no easy way to check each other out. Had they been permitted to talk with each other, it would not have taken very long to reduce tension and to find some basis for at least a modicum of trust.

This experience in nonverbal interaction offers a clue both about trust and about self-disclosure. In this respect humans are not much different from other species. Animals become suddenly alerted at the presence of another animal and begin to sniff at each other cautiously. It takes a while for them even under the most favorable circumstances to become less vigilant and more relaxed.

Disclosures from the hidden quadrant (Q3) are ordinarily done gradually and reciprocally. Under special circumstances such as a crisis or an emergency, the acquaintance process may be speeded up. A regional power failure, an earthquake, an acute illness in a neighborhood, or an accident may radically change interpersonal processes and produce new disclosures. The releasing effect of public crises puzzles many people who cannot understand why a catastrophe may have such satisfying effect on interpersonal exchanges.

It would be of value to examine more closely what occurs as two or more persons grow in trust and become more open about themselves. Perhaps an element of risk-taking paces the process of change. By risk I mean the chance you take in having your feelings hurt, such as becoming more anxious or embarrassed, insulted, belittled or in other ways offended. There are other kinds of psychological assaults that make one a bit wary. How much does it take to make you feel foolish, irritated, annoyed, angry, ashamed, or guilty? Waiters, bellboys, and others who rely heavily for their income on eliciting gratuities from customers are sometimes highly skilled in letting a patron know that he will not be let off easy if he violates the level of tipping. Or perhaps experience with the general public has not always been pleasant and the waiters and bellboys have had to learn to protect themselves. In brief, there are real psychological hazards in even the most perfunctory relationships and the hazards are increased to the extent that one's openness makes him vulnerable.

What about the risks of not being open, of not disclosing? Is it true that one is psychologically safer by keeping his third quadrant to himself? Isn't it foolish to let people know what you feel and think?

The answer is no, quite the contrary. I say this unequivocally even though there must be times when everyone regrets having been too transparent. I cannot recall a single group of persons who came together to learn about people, about themselves, and about groups who did not discover that they were too closed off from people in everyday

life in their families, on their jobs, and with friends. Sometimes this discovery is expressed in words like feeling lonely, isolated, alienated.
Most of the time participants experience deep satisfaction with their
feelings of greater openness and intimacy after working through some
of their common group problems. They begin to see direct connections
between their initial behavior in a group and their behavior at home.

Another set of risks involved in not sharing selectively from your
hidden third quadrant has to do with learning about your own self. As
mentioned earlier, if to know yourself is of interest to you and if appropriate self-disclosure to others is an integral part of the learning-
about-self process, the risk you run in not being open is clear.

In addition, there is the risk of loss of personal flexibility. As mentioned in the original description of the Johari Window, it takes energy
and attention to hold back reactions. Spontaneity is reduced and others
then see you as more inflexible. It also takes considerable energy to set
the face into a rigid mold, a mask, and then to hold the mask in place.

But feelings and expressions, not only of face but of the whole body
and of the voice as well, are difficult to disguise and perhaps impossible
to control totally. Sometimes in holding back, the best you can do is to
distort what comes through, thereby interfering with communication
and with other interpersonal transactions.

Finally, the risks of being more open and more transparent must be
borne not only for the satisfactions and enjoyment of people and of
self, but for increased realization of self. Lest that last phrase slip by
as just another platitude, I'd like to rephrase it something like this.
Your talent and your potentials have a better chance of being developed
if you as a person have access to your own feelings, your imagination,
and your fantasy. If you can be open and free even with but one other
person there is greater likelihood that you can be in touch with self.
In Johari terms, *a change in any quadrant affects all quadrants*, and
since you have direct awareness in the first and third quadrants, the
behavior and motivation here are subject to your control. Regardless
of other risks, the greatest risk therefore would come from not exercising the awareness and control you do have.

A middle-aged woman who holds an important job and has a pleasant, dignified appearance became increasingly dissatisfied with her

behavior in a learning group. Frequent misunderstandings of what she tried to say plus patronizing reactions from others bothered her. It took quite a while before she became aware of the fact that she was overcontrolling her own reactions to what was going on. She was finally stung by the remark made by an influential member who lumped her together with two other persons who were seen as "nice," meaning bland and ineffectual. She had enough confidence in the group by this time to express her annoyance in what was for her a strong outburst. To her surprise she found that this free expression made the group take notice of her in a new way. She then admitted that she felt she had to be diplomatic at all times, that she thought her face was too transparent, and that it was all she could do to try to keep people from knowing what was going on within. It was only then that she learned in new exchanges with others that she could well afford the risk of being herself more. Further, she became aware that her expressive face, instead of being an unfortunate handicap, was actually a lively and colorful aspect of her whole bearing. In the next few days she was much more relaxed and more expressive too. She seemed to have shed a tightness of visage; she acknowledged feeling freer and more buoyant than she had for a long time. She became a more active person as well as a more enjoyable group member.

There are certain persons who plunge into a relationship. (Samuel Culbert [1967] refers to these as revealers. As I use the term, a plunger is a high revealer.) Lewin (1948) has observed that Americans are far more casual and open about the acquaintance process than Europeans. He does add, however, that once a European develops a close relationship, he is more apt to go deeper both in his disclosures and in his involvement than the American. But surely in both populations there are the plungers who, relative to the general norm, tend to be both more open and more trusting than others. Though I do not have the evidence at hand I would guess that where this openness is expressed with due consideration for what is going on with the other, there is indeed apt to be a quicker development in the pattern of relationships. However, for many the plunger or quick self-discloser is anathema, to be avoided at all costs. A plunger when he proceeds without due consideration for you is one who discloses the hidden or private area at a rate that usually is too rapid for your comfort.

Since it is possible to move too slowly or too rapidly in disclosing Q3, what principles govern appropriate disclosure?

The experiment on nonverbal interaction (Appendix 2) again offers clues. In dyads A and B and C, the reactions of S's to each other tended to converge even though their rating scales were kept confidential. Subjects in dyads A and B were able to perceive and to react to each other even without verbal communication in a way that suggested reciprocal feelings. In dyad B, for instance, subject Sj started by rating Sb at plus six on a like–dislike scale and before the first session was over moved to plus eight. Subject Sb, however, started cooly, rating her feelings at plus two. In the next meeting, Sj dropped from plus six to plus four, and Sb rose from plus two to four. Though there were other variations in the five meetings, there was an over-all tendency for the reactions to converge, so that at the end they were both at the same plus eight on the scale.

In dyad A, the differences in rating were small throughout the five meetings. Dyad C was exceptional in that subject Sm held a rigid reaction, plus nine, in every meeting; subject Sm had the highest authoritarian score among all the subjects and gave other indications of personality difficulty manifested in an inordinate desire to please everybody. Even with her, in the restricted atmosphere of the experiment (no direct communication was permitted), the other subject eventually increased her like score to converge with Sm's on the final meeting.

In a study of "self-disclosure and interpersonal effectiveness," Halverson and Shore (1969) evaluated fifty-three Peace Corps trainees on a series of personality dimensions, including authoritarianism, sociometric choice, interpersonal flexibility and adaptability, and conceptual complexity. The latter is a measure of ability to appreciate alternative ways of viewing a social situation. Self-disclosure was negatively correlated with authoritarianism and positively correlated with conceptual complexity. "A person of a higher level of conceptual complexity interacts in an interdependent manner (i.e., assuming mutuality and equality in relationships), whereas one at a low level presumably interacts unilaterally (e.g., dominant and submissive roles). It follows that there should be more openness in communicating to others in an interdependent rather than a unilateral interaction" (1969, p. 216). In addition conceptual complexity correlates significantly with interpersonal flexibility and general adaptability, in the findings of this research.

Halverson and Shore also found that "self-disclosure assumes importance in the development of more stable and less superficial interpersonal relationships" (p. 216). That is, the trainees disclosed self in growing relationships selectively. Another interesting finding by the researchers supports the idea that intelligence itself (as measured by two different intelligence tests) is not related to openness or accessibility. Other personality variables, such as those mentioned above, determine the degree of self-disclosure. It should be noted that conceptual complexity as the researchers define it (the capacity to process interpersonal information in a flexible way) is not significantly correlated with intelligence.

The question remains: When is self-disclosure appropriate?

In an earlier discussion bearing on Q3 it was pointed out that the person has some choice in disclosing himself because the hidden area is known to self and not to others. Principles governing what is disclosed, where and when and to whom, have only recently begun to be studied systematically. These questions bear closely on the meaning and quality of interpersonal relations, and are tied in with wide-ranging issues in the teaching-learning process, psychotherapy, leadership, encounter group practice, and intraorganizational life. It is apparent that what is considered appropriate self-disclosure will vary with each individual, his life style, his social environment, and other important and unique variables. Still it may be of value to characterize appropriate self-disclosure through a series of hunches from which testable hypotheses may be drawn. Self-disclosure is appropriate:

1. *When it is a function of the ongoing relationship.* What one shares with another belongs in the particular relationship; it is not a random or isolated act.

2. *When it occurs reciprocally.* This implies that there is some degree of interdependency and mutuality involved.

3. *When it is timed to fit what is happening.* The self-disclosure grows out of the experience that is going on between or among the persons involved. The timing and sequence are important.

4. *When it concerns what is going on within and between persons in the present.* Some account is taken of the behavior and feelings of the participants individually and of the persons collectively. There is recog-

nition of the relationship as an emergent phenomenon in addition to the individual selves.

5. *When it moves by relatively small increments.* What is revealed does not drastically change or restructure the relationship. The implication is that a relationship is built gradually except in rare and special cases.

6. *When it is confirmable by the other person.* Some system is worked out between the persons to validate reception of that which has been disclosed.

7. *When account is taken of the effect disclosure has on the other person(s).* The disclosure has not only been received; there is evidence of its effect on the receiver.

8. *When it creates a reasonable risk.* If the feeling or behavior were really unknown to the other, it may have been withheld for a reason bearing on differences which have yet to be faced by the participants.

9. *When it is speeded up in a crisis.* A serious conflict jeopardizing the structure of the relationship may require that more Q3 material be quickly revealed to heal the breach or help in the reshaping of the relationship.

10. *When the context is mutually shared.* The assumptions underlying the social context suggest that there is enough in common to sustain the disclosure.

The fact that persons will sometimes use casual meetings as the social setting for disclosing rather important personal information suggests that the need to reveal personal matters is not always gratified. Persons may be trapped in social relations such that the perceived risk prevents freer interaction. Since most social relations do not have built-in conditions for clarifying the bases for risks or the nature of mutual entrapment, stalemate sets in. The individual looks elsewhere, hardly aware that he is in a trapped state or that he can work out of it. Sometimes a bartender or plane passenger can help by just listening. More often than not, such contacts with friendly strangers are less than satisfying and the individual is still in a stalemate in his usual social relations. Encounter groups at times offer an opportunity to learn about characteristic hangups, with a chance for new awareness and different behavioral experience to carry over to back-home situations. Again, the encounter group is not a panacea, but it does demonstrate repeatedly that under competent guidance many participants learn significant things about people and groups in general and about their own relationships in particular.

The Explicit versus the Literal

To be explicit is not the same as being literal in human interaction. The Johari model calls attention to dilemmas arising out of limited awareness and illustrates the effects of disclosure and concealment of thinking and feeling. The model leads to emphasis on the power and meaning of openness in interaction with others. Reducing obscurity and ambiguity may call for explicitness, but not necessarily literalness. It is not necessary to spell everything out. No one wants all that concreteness, except on those special occasions when the moment has too much at stake and when everything has suddenly become unhinged, and even then what is wanted is a special, literal piece of behavior. Perhaps a dialogue but not a diagnosis, not dialectics. Action, like language, can be explicit or literal, sometimes both, sometimes neither.

☐ *"Silence is full of the words we never uttered."* — A political prisoner in Portugal to his beloved

Nuance and subtlety need not be sacrificed for openness. Ever-widening areas may be brought into awareness without reducing shadings and gradations. The more that is understood about people, the more complexities appear.

Explicitness in interaction may reduce ambiguousness only to reveal new states which are inherently ambivalent. For example, the quality of an employee's respect for his supervisor may turn out to be less a feeling of esteem and more one of fear. And the fear may be compounded of a dependency-independency pattern of feelings in which the employee is caught, at this stage in his development.

Living relationships cannot be spelled out in full detail because they are inexhaustible. Perhaps this is what Oliver W. Holmes had in mind when he said, "Life is not adding up a sum. It's painting a picture." The act of making all relationships literal is to constrict and terminate whatever possibilities were there.

It would be interesting to study the death of close relationships to see to what extent they expire of natural causes and to what extent their dissolution comes about through psychological violence. In the former, people grow apart. In the latter, the blind and hidden quadrants are violated or disclosed and made painfully literal. The fact that it may be possible to learn from this kind of forced exchange is small solace to the victims. Their settings, even the legal and blood ties of families, are usually inadequate to sustain the break-up. In the abstract, it may be true that no relationship need be torn apart irreversibly. Given the right circumstances of time, persons, and skill, ties may be healed and even strengthened. In a century marked by all kinds of war and violence this may seem visionary, if not foolish. But it is there, I believe, in society's fourth quadrant.

When the Subjective Is the True

The most important questions in any relationship are, "What does he think of me?" and "How does he feel toward me?" and "How does he see me?" So crucial are these questions that R. D. Laing, for instance, develops a system to describe sanity and madness in terms of just such interpersonal perception. Since every perception is also an interpretation, the objectively valid is important only to the extent that it affects the interpretation. But much of what goes into an interpretation of behavior is only remotely related to that behavior. And the same behavior may be seen differently by different people and often in opposite ways, as described by Laing (1966, p.11): "I act in a way that is *cautious* to me, but *cowardly* to you. You act in a way that is *courageous* to you, but *foolhardy* to me. She sees herself as *vivacious*, but he sees her as *superficial*. He sees himself as *friendly*, she sees him as *seductive*. She sees herself as *reserved*, he sees her as *haughty and aloof*. He sees himself as *gallant*, she sees him as *phoney*. She sees herself as *feminine*, he sees her as *helpless and dependent*. He sees himself as *masculine*, she sees him as *overbearing and dominating*."

Because of the endless possibilities and limitless doubts (see, for instance, Gibb, 1961, p. 143) involved in interpersonal perception, the act of interpersonal confirmation is of special importance. To confirm one another is to authenticate as valid how we perceive each other. It means to give some degree of certainty to that previously regarded as doubtful. It is one of the most important ways of alleviating anxiety. Interpersonal confirmation means concurring on interpersonal perception. There is the relief that comes with corroboration of what one is, what one thinks, and what one feels. One is even strengthened to the point where one need pay less attention to what one is and release energy toward what one can become. In short, to confirm another person is to enhance his prospects of growing in line with his potentials.

Trust and Tolerance

In a discussion with Tillich several years ago, a well-known psychologist commented that granting another person freedom to be was the most important thing in a helping relationship. Tillich agreed and added, "But who can grant that much freedom?" (Though the words may not be verbatim they are, I believe, an accurate expression of the ideas exchanged.) The definition of trust as expressed by Charlotte Buhler in O'Donovan's paper (1965) is useful: "the expectation of the opportunity to function and to become in a world which provides support and freedom."

The Tillich comment stimulated me to reexamine the way trust is ordinarily used. I found that the most common abuse of the term "to trust" was to confound it with "to tolerate." A client, a subordinate, a colleague, a student, a friend, a spouse, a child, can tell when he is offered freedom and when he is being tolerated. He senses that tolerance is merely a moratorium on disapproval. Tolerance would not be so bad if the one who grants it were not trying to palm it off as freedom. It's like the clunk of a lead nickel in the blind man's cup; he knows at once that you're not doing him much good, while you make it appear to others and perhaps to yourself that you're a generous guy. Offering support with tolerance is nice, and perhaps that is as far as most of us go, ordinarily. But this is not to be confused with trust which requires the "opportunity to function and to become" as well as support.

In his investigations of qualities of effective psychotherapists, O'Donovan (1965) was surprised to find that detachment in interaction with clients was an important variable. "Some time before, I had been counseled by a wiser psychologist, Mrs. Judy Allee, that effective therapy involved a willingness on the part of the therapist to 'let the patient go to hell in a wheel-barrow.' This advice at first appeared harsh and unfeeling. Then gradually I began to realize the relationship between detachment and trust."

Then O'Donovan offers Buhler's definition of trust and added, "I began to realize that, like many parents and like paternal psychoanalysts, I had been emphasizing the support and neglecting the freedom." O'Donovan concludes, "The separateness of therapist and client is recognized, along with the right of each to function and become within his own value system. Perhaps the findings that detachment rather than togetherness or sympathy is relatively favored by [the more effective] therapists has some bearing on this problem. ... The client may learn that it is possible to have a deeply meaningful relationship without conforming to the values of the significant other."

The Quandary

Make a list of friends and relations who tolerate you as you are. Now make another list of those who trust you to become in your own way something else. It is easy to predict which list will be longer; for many, sad to say, there is no one on the second list. If it is true that you can become more of what you potentially can become only in relationship with others, then we can understand how universal is the trust-relationship hunger. Trust means to be in a state of mutual and reciprocal interest *and* to be free to become. It is the *sine qua non* for self-actualization.

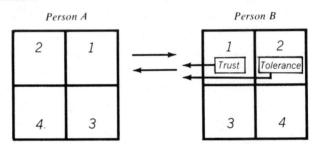

Misery in a relationship means to expect trust and to get tolerance. In Johari terms there is a feeling of trust in Q1 but a tolerance attitude appears in Q2. In the *A-B* friendship, *B* believes he genuinely trusts *A* and as far as he is aware he offers trust to *A* in his open quadrant 1. However, *A* gets "tolerance" messages from *B's* blind quadrant. *B* is not so free that he can grant *A* the sanction, to say nothing of the opportunity, to become something else, to change in some way. *B needs A to stay the way he is and not to change.* If *A* reciprocates to *B* a similar double message, then the relationship may be fixed at a somewhat cool level. There would be a tendency to reinforce each other in believing the relationship to be something it is not. This may be acceptable and suitable to both *A* and *B*. Trouble arises when either changes or puts the relationship to a test. If the change goes beyond the tolerance level of the other, then the relationship becomes spotted with criticism and bickering and may break off altogether. Often, the change may simply result in dilution of friendship; the two people see less and less of each other. If the change is such as to produce an abrupt withdrawal by either, it may be seen as a rejection or betrayal. "I liked him, trusted him, and now look how he behaves."

Others who are in some relationship with you probably do want you to change. Your friends, spouse, and colleagues are always attempting to influence you. Strangely, they may be disappointed when you do change in directions they had advocated. A colleague may urge his officemate to do more scholarly things and then find he has lost an important relationship when his friend becomes absorbed in research. A mother may keep after her daughter to bring her friends home and then discover she cannot tolerate groups of teenagers. And spouses are always discovering that changes may bring unpredictable consequences.

A trusting relationship would appear to be less stable. There would be a need to come to terms with the changes in either or both persons. There would be a continuing risk that change would make the other person less suitable, less needed.

> Martha and Bess were good friends for many years while Bess was in college. Martha had her own family; she found Bess charming, interesting, and rather immature. She helped Bess through a number of social crises and Bess was genuinely grateful for Martha's friendship.
>
> Bess married a mechanic who had a small shop in a nearby town. She saw Martha less frequently but always as a valuable friend. Slowly, Bess changed. She took over office responsibilities in her husband's shop, and they became well established in the social life of the town. Martha's visits to Bess became less frequent. She complained to mutual friends that Bess had become less interesting, a more limited, provincial person. Bess was a disappointment and Martha felt sorry for her. Others who had known both women could not understand what Martha was talking about. Bess led a more versatile and varied life than ever in the town and she enjoyed helping her husband with the paper work and the social demands connected with his business. One day Bess called on Martha for assistance. She had had a second miscarriage and a bad anemic condition. Also her husband had expanded his business and was now operating a supply store *and* the shop. He was busy most of their waking hours and sometimes on weekends as well.
>
> Martha was magnanimous. She was a helpful dynamo taking care of Bess's chores, social obligations, and even occasional meals. And

there was no doubt that the friendship seemed as strong and as rich as ever. The two had long talks in which Martha gently chastised Bess for the way she was denying herself so many advantages of a fuller life in the large university community. It was only then that Bess began to see that Martha could not accept the changes in her. Bess tried a few times to let Martha know how different she felt about the many cultural activities they used to enjoy together. She tried without much success to express what it meant to run the little office at the shop. Her description of her husband's way of life was received with a bland and somewhat patronizing understanding by Martha. Bess was greatly relieved by Martha's assistance, but after the first few visits, she was depressed at the end of each stay. At first she attributed her distressed frame of mind to the anemia, but the physician said she was doing well and could soon go about her regular work. And then she realized that with each visit and talk with Martha she felt stifled. The conversation rippled with disagreements about little things until a particularly unpleasant exchange about preparing a salad dressing. Martha left, but not before she informed Bess how insensitive and ungrateful Bess had become.

A Way of Looking at Love

Some time ago I wrote myself a note on a matchbook cover. It said, "People come together in groups to learn to trust in order to become, to see more of their own uniqueness among the individual differences."

This was written while I was in a group process lab, and I forgot about it. Sometime later I found an article on love by Nelson N. Foote (1962). When his friends and colleagues learned that he was working on this topic, they reacted in one of four categories: cynical, joking, sentimental, and matter of fact. Few were matter of fact; those who were pointed out that the subject was not academically respectable and that at best it could not be dealt with scientifically.

Nelson Foote defines love as "that relationship between one person and another which is most conducive to the optimal development of both. This optimal development is to be measured practically in the growth of competence in interpersonal relations." A bit later he adds, "Trust and appreciation accumulate through proven results as indexed in mutual personal development."

I went back to my matchbook cover. So that's what was going on in these groups: of course, learning and trust and love go together. There was so much excess freight carried in the four letter word that for ordinary communication it may have lost its usefulness. At any rate, I became more convinced of the interconnectedness of these large concepts when I found Buhler's definition of trust as, "the expectation of the opportunity to function and to become in a world which provides support and freedom" (in O'Donovan, 1965).

An encounter group would have to meet "the expectation of the opportunity" if it were to work in accordance with its purpose. Still I was unclear about the goal "to function and to become." I had seen groups functioning and people moving and changing in accordance with their inherent tendencies, but there was still much ambiguity. I found value in returning to the self-concept as a way of talking about "becoming." And John Cumming's ideas drawn from his work with patients were, it seemed to me, as universally applicable as the idea of trust itself (Cumming, 1960, p. 113):

I have proposed that much of what Langer has spoken of as the "sheer expression of ideas" or symbolic activity for its own sake, is in normal people, the function of constantly rebuilding the self-concept, of offering this self-concept to others for ratification, and of accepting or rejecting the self-conceptual offerings of others.

I have assumed therefore, that the self-concept is continually to be rebuilt if we are to exist as people and not as objects, and in the main the self-concept is rebuilt in communicative activity.

Buber (1957) addressed himself to the same central issue when he stated that "... a society may be termed human in the measure to which its members confirm one another." Erikson (1951) observed, "Hard though it be to achieve, the sense of identity is the individual's only safeguard against the lawlessness of his biological drives and the authority of an over-weening conscience." And in another paragraph, Erikson noted, "It has been observed by those who know young people well that high school age boys and girls often use each other's company for an endless verbal examination of what the other thinks, feels, and wants to do. In other words, these attachments are one means of defining one's identity.

In an ingenious symposium entitled "Therapy by Design" (Good, Siegel, and Bay, 1965) psychologists and psychiatrists invited a distinguished architect, Richard Neutra, to discuss relationships between the physical structure of a mental institution and the effect induced on patients. Neutra affirmed what most people know intuitively: that the physical dimensions of a room, a corridor, or a window all had demonstrable effects on a person. The person's total environment communicates continuously to him messages of value, worth, and regard. And referring to the rapid and planless ways in which we destroy old buildings and neighborhoods for purposes of real estate development, Neutra observed that, "To lose one's town, to lose one's past, is to lose one's self." Perhaps here we have another clue to the current epidemic of meaninglessness, despair, fear of death, or mere boredom. It would appear then that interaction with one's environment has a bearing on being and becoming more human as well as on interaction with other persons. This is something artists and others have always known. It seems to me that residential labs on group and interpersonal relations held in quiet, handsome surroundings confirm and nourish the inspiriting effect of the human interaction itself.

Perhaps the idea of love in a learning group is still not precisely focused. But the idea helps explain why there is wide-scale, if not universal, need for interpersonal learning. Here are other terms for love, if this term still seems misleading: people need people to confirm each other, to help in the constant rebuilding of the self-concept, and to grow in competence in interpersonal relations.

On Feeling Understood

At the core of human interaction is the experience of "really feeling understood." Adrian L. van Kaam (1959) studied this question empirically with 120 college men and women and 245 high school seniors. Using a direct approach ("Describe how you feel when you feel that you are really being understood by somebody") as a way of exploring the issue phenomenologically, van Kaam found remarkable consistency in this most subjective experience. The feeling of satisfaction, for example, was reported by 99 per cent of the subjects, feeling initially relieved from experiential loneliness by 89 per cent, feeling safe in the relationship by 91 per cent.

Van Kaam describes the phenomenon in this way: "The experience of 'really feeling understood' is a perceptual-emotional Gestalt: A subject, perceiving that a person co-experiences what things mean to the subject and accepts him, feels, initially, relief from experiential loneliness, and gradually, safe experiential communion with that person and with that which the subject perceives this person to represent" (1959, p. 69).

Asking my own students the same question, I received quite similiar responses, such as, "I felt as if a great weight had been taken off my back." ". . . a feeling of wholeness, openness." "It was sort of a relief, emotional, mental, physical." "I felt a sense of universality or oneness or a part of everything." "I thought that I was in love." ". . . like diving into a pool and finding it warm and comforting." "For an instant I had lost the feeling of being alone."

In Johari terms, the person who feels understood receives acknowledgment that what is known to self is known to the other (Q1) in a way that does not add strain or inner violence. In other words, what goes on in the hidden, blind, and unknown quadrants is not again jarred nor unduly challenged. The person receives momentary but convincing affirmation of what he feels he is and the way he perceives the world around him at that moment.

A form of cruelty in human interaction is to deliberately misunderstand the other. It is not simply misunderstanding however; rather it is misunderstanding based on understanding. A good fight or argument is one in which you come away feeling you've exchanged differences, but that the other person understands what you feel and mean. A nasty fight is one in which the other deliberately misconstrues what you think. He acts in a manner that says you are not coming through at all the way you think you are. In a group, when a number of participants in collusion do this to an individual, the effect can be rather devastating. Yet so powerful is the experience of feeling understood that even if only one other person expresses understanding, the individual under attack gains enormous strength (Asch, 1956).

But one does not have to be unfairly attacked to be in need of understanding. Apparently, to feel deeply understood is a relatively unusual event occurring in special relationships. For many, it is a rare and precious experience, savored for a long time after it takes place. It may be no exaggeration to say that every human contact is an occasion when one or more persons may have a "feeling understood" experience. Every interaction also offers someone the chance to be understanding.

There are two major sources of anxiety and despair and though they have an interactive effect, it is useful to look at them separately. One stems from inner life as a function of growing up and the struggle to become a person. The relevant crises are personal and no one can evade them without significant psychological loss. When the crises are successfully resolved, the individual has a chance to be a whole person and unique. Even the successful one, however, cannot escape pain, for as Tillich (1959, p. 23) states, "... the more original a man is, the deeper is his anxiety; but if he can stand it, he has preserved his freedom and reached highest self-actualization." There is a greater likelihood that he can stand it if he has a sufficient number of occasions for feeling understood along the way.

The other major source of anxiety and despair is evident in crises in society, a breakdown in the way social and community institutions meet human needs. The step from despair to violence may not be a very large one under certain conditions of real and perceived social injustice. When it appears to a person in the community that he is being ignored, rejected, denied, and excluded, it is not surprising that he will feel abused *and* not understood. It is for the good of all that those who feel so deprived not remain silent. However, if understanding is offered *in place of* the needed changes in society, if real opportunities are still not available, then we should not be surprised to find that the person feels cheated as well as abused. A man needs to know that choices are open to him before he can dream of realizing his potential. For many, the immediate problem, as Reiff (1966) states, is self-determination rather than self-actualization. Both self-determination and self-actualization are important: it is usually impossible to say where one begins and the other ends. Hence some opportunity for feeling understood is valuable all along. In the community, work groups, and in industrial organizations, the key value is participation and some reasonable degree of self-determination. In interpersonal relations the emphasis is more on personal and emotional satisfaction.

I suppose the search in our time for meaning has at its center this kind of human interaction, this quality of human understanding. Watzlawick (1967, p. 265) writes, "the absence of meaning is the horror of existential nothingness. It is that subjective state in which reality has receded or disappeared altogether, and with it any awareness of self and others." Where the context of living encourages impersonalness and uninvolvement, as in so many institutions and places around us, there a feeling of meaninglessness tends to be epidemic.

Efforts over time to increase man's understanding of the world and of life have apparently not significantly reduced his doubts about meaningfulness in the universe. Perhaps it is true that unless he derives from human interaction the special quality of feeling understood, he will suffer the despair of meaninglessness no matter what he achieves and how well he understands everything else. Feeling understood appears then to be a necessary though perhaps not a sufficient condition for man to come to terms with the world and with himself. Hypothetically, every man can offer the gift of really feeling understood to someone, provided he can relate with him in a way that makes it possible to co-experience what is going on within.

Being understanding, when one is able to do so, is rewarding in its own right even though it is not the same as feeling understood. But when it is mutual, when you and I understand as well as feel understood simultaneously, then for that moment the world is home and bread is baking in the oven.

Personal Values and the Unknown*

How the individual comes to terms with the significant unknowns in his life is crucial to the qualities inherent in his system of personal values. In fact, they are his values. The questions which follow are typical of the kind we all face; the implicit and explicit ways in which we confront questions such as these are the values we live by.

1. Here is a stranger. I know nothing about him. How shall I confront him? Can I trust him?

2. What happens upon death? No one seems to have any clear information. How shall I face the prospect of its inevitability?

3. How much of a risk can I afford to take in my business or in my profession? Shall I stay within the safe limits of the known and the predictable or dare I venture toward an undefined goal involving many unknowns?

4. How free and open can I be? How much of myself do I really permit myself to express, to be, in my most intimate relationships? In how many different relationships can I and will I be this way? In other words, how much do I feel I need to conceal in close relationships?

5. To what extent do I really permit myself to become more aware of those aspects of myself which are still unknown to me, those potentials still unrealized?

6. At what point do I restrict the possibilities for becoming more intimately acquainted with the real world outside my immediate self? Not merely open but actively probing? Or, how much curiosity stirs me to know, to have more knowledge and understanding of the world.

7. Am I free enough to tolerate, if not to enjoy, the spontaneous and unpredictable in myself and in others?

8. Where do I stand in relation to the symbols and rituals which go back to my childhood and to ancient times, the meanings of which are never to be exhausted? How do I relate myself to the vaguely known past and the unknown future so that these have significant bearing on and can be seen to exist in the present?

---

*From "A Way of Looking at Values" by Joseph Luft in *Human Relations Training News*, vol. 8, no. 1, spring, 1964, pp. 6-7, published by the National Training Laboratories. Reprinted by permission.

As mentioned, these questions are a few among many which can be drawn up and which have a powerful bearing on who we are and what we stand for. Most if not all of these issues are of course dealt with implicitly, and the individual is often unaware that he stands in a particular relation to them. But his actual behavior on these matters speaks unequivocally. Each of us is put to the test over and over again, and one need but stop and observe to determine the mode of our personal positions or the positions of others with regard to the various unknowns.

Structural Intervention*

In this paper I should like to examine the meaning and use of structural intervention in laboratory training. A structural intervention is usually initiated by a staff member and calls for a change in group form or procedure on a trial basis. While there are interesting new types of structural interventions, there is nothing novel about the concept. Consultation exercises, lectures, and buzz groups are structural interventions, familiar activities in the staff member's repertoire. Cluster design, movement sessions, and ephemeral groups are examples of more recent structural interventions in laboratory work.

The purpose of the more usual type of intervention is to call attention to an ongoing process in the group—between persons or within an individual. A structural intervention, however, is usually *not* directed to a particular individual or to a set of individuals or to a group process. It is a suggestion to the group for a temporary change in form or procedure in order to facilitate unfreezing and thereby to heighten interaction and new learning. For example, one group became bogged down as every effort to work was trumped and blocked by its members. Instead of calling attention to this process, a perfectly acceptable intervention, I proposed that the group split into two subgroups on a self-selective basis. The shift took place quickly; chairs and other furniture were moved, and the subgroups became immersed in a flood of new interactions and new talk. When they returned to the group as a whole,

* From "Structural Intervention" by Joseph L*i*ft in *Human Relations Training News,* vol. 10, no. 2, summer, 1966, pp. 1-2, published by the National Training Laboratories. Reprinted by permission.

one could observe at once the infusion of new data and feelings. They talked about the basis of self-selections, the new freedom they felt, and looked more boldly at the reasons for their stalemate.

The group may or may not follow the trainer's suggestion. He may be ignored or challenged. As usual, the trainer stands ready to face the consequences. In my experience, the participants take a rather pragmatic view of these suggestions and quickly decide for themselves whether the change is useful. Charges of manipulation are openly met and checked out as a function of the development of trust. Eventually, participants learn to make their own structural interventions.

Structural interventions are powerful things—in one stroke they may change many process elements such as atmosphere, persons confronted, and the group's focus of attention. A successful structural intervention may be noted by what follows, by what happens, and whether or not it helps generate a problem-solving set. Participants become aware that they can influence their fate, that they can find new ways to change if they want to change.

In most groups, members become bound and limited by the basic struggles of group life and are rarely in a position, initially, to perceive relationships between structural elements and group processes. We know that groups may split into factions on issues dealing with direction, order, and structure. The real issue is not more or less structure. Rather, it is a question of appropriateness of structure. Since participants are usually limited by their experience, it comes as a new idea to devise and to adapt structural changes to the unique work of laboratory group learning.

Group structural elements include such things as number of persons, number of subunits, composition, movement, physical setting, task setting, and time limits. Selection principles for groups and subgroups could be widely varied; for example, volunteers, consultation arrangements, intergroup projects, self-selection, ephemeral groups, grouping by occupation, sex, language, special experience, intragroup focus, organizational projects, and matched groups. The last-mentioned are matched in the same sense that milieu therapy is a matched arrangement. For example, a supportive person is matched with a person who needs support. Roger Harrison (1965) has described composition models in which participants were classified according to behavioral dimensions and grouped with others so that members were of value to one another naturally in the learning process.

Structural Intervention As Improvised Design

Structural intervention calls for a particular kind of improvisation. Perhaps invention is a better word for it, because once a skillful improvisation is made, it can sometimes be recognized as a unique design and reused as the need arises. I should like to underline the last phrase, "as the need arises," because few things are as disconcerting as a good idea in the wrong place at the wrong time.

It becomes clear after a while that the original design of the workshop, the schedule, and the over-all plan are integrally related to the later structural interventions. The initial design of the laboratory is, after all, based on a set of assumptions and hypotheses. A large number of imponderables are assessed, together with some fairly well-known expectations about how a particular group of persons will function. There is always a need, it seems to me, to adapt a design to a group as the nature of the group and its unique composition and problems become better known to the staff members. Rigidity in staff planning is at least as serious a problem as any of those encountered by the participants. Structural interventions can go a long way toward the readaptation of a group to optimal conditions of work and learning.

A group is a social nexus when, through the experience of its members with one another, a complex of forces evolves and within which the persons are enmeshed. Thoughts and feelings and fantasies about one another and about the group grow and develop. Yet each member has limited awareness of these forces and may actually be trapped by them. By structural intervention, a deliberate effort is made to break momentarily the social nexus which permits new leeway in the perceptions and feelings and fantasies so that the trapped individuals may be able to move psychologically.

A change in structure will actually change the stimulus value of persons which, in turn, will modify, to some extent, the inner life of the participants. In this respect, the use of movement (see Appendix 3) may be considered a special class of intervention.

A particularly dramatic form of intervention is to instruct a group in the use of alone time. (I am indebted to Barry Oshry for this idea. However, its particular implementation and interpretation here are my responsibility.) A brief period of time is set aside for members to leave the group and to move outside or to another part of the building. The idea is to invoke a period of solitude. No talking and no interaction are permitted. The participant is alone with his thoughts, feelings, and fantasies. One variant of this intervention is to instruct members to limit their attention to a small patch of earth or sky, or a tree or a plant. In this way, the nature and pattern of stimuli are changed and limited. Participants soon begin to externalize their inner worlds of feelings and discover that the physical world, in its ambiguous form, takes on some of the qualities of their fantasies and feelings. Thus one member, reporting back after his alone-time experience, told of seeing harassed insects struggling and fighting for survival. Another reported that in watching a clump of trees he felt very lonely and separated from the flow of life and activity. Still another was awed at the play of colors and forms in a few small leaves on a branch. Again, upon return after but a quarter of an hour, a marked change in group atmosphere and a feeling of sadness mixed with a basic concern for all living things were apparent. It was as if all the unessentials, the trivia of group life, were temporarily removed.

Social Invention

I believe that structural intervention can be a form of social invention, as mentioned above, and that it is an important step toward the appreciation and understanding of group life. There are rapid changes in social forms. (Matthew B. Miles [1963] makes a valuable contribution by spelling out the nature and endless varieties of temporary systems all around us. He examines the self-defeating resistance to change within systems and points up the need for greater understanding of the change process and the value of experience with innovative temporary systems.) With the dissolution of structures upon which we heretofore relied to meet human needs and to enhance interpersonal learning, structural intervention will be increasingly important as an applied art and as a subject for scientific investigation.

Laboratory groups provide an excellent setting in which structural intervention can be studied. Groups which make up much of our society are subject to the same basic processes as laboratory groups and, as such, are amenable to the effects of structural intervention. Systematic research on groups outside the laboratory is, of course, essential, but the study of structural intervention in group laboratories could lead the way.

APPENDIX 2

On Nonverbal Interaction*

Introduction

This is a study of nonverbal interaction, an attempt at finding ways of measuring and understanding what takes place affectively between two persons in a nonverbal task-free situation.

Dyadic interaction is clearly one of the fundamental processes in clinical and social psychology, and personality theorists reveal their basic differences when they attempt to explain what takes place in a dyad and why. Some account must be made of large classes of variables, such as what the subject brings to the situation, the context in which interaction occurs (see, for instance, Luft, 1953), what the persons perceive (Luft, 1957), the conscious and unconscious needs involved, and the variables in the behavioral interchange itself. The problem of the researcher is to hold down the number of variables so that some sense can be made of the behavior observed. However, this

---

* From "On Nonverbal Interaction" by Joseph Luft in *The Journal of Psychology,* 63:261-68, 1966. Reprinted by permission.

is not quite as simple as it sounds for, as Cronbach (1958) remarked after examining the results of many studies in this field, the findings are "interesting, significant and exasperatingly inconsistent."

One clue about the significance of meeting persons for the first time comes from Charles H. Cooley (1902, p. 207):

> There is a vague excitement of the social self more general than any particular emotion or sentiment. Thus the mere presence of people, a "sense of other persons" and an awareness of their observation, often causes a vague discomfort, doubt and tension. One feels that there is a social image of himself lurking about, and not knowing what it is he is obscurely alarmed. Many people, perhaps most, feel more or less agitation and embarrassment under the observation of strangers, and for some even sitting in the same room with unfamiliar or uncongenial people is harassing and exhausting. It is well known, for instance, that a visit from a stranger would often cost Darwin his night's sleep and many similar examples could be collected from the records of men of letters. At this point, however, it is evident that we approach the borders of mental pathology.

Problems and Method

Basically what I and colleagues did in the present study was to bring together two subjects (S's) who did not know each other and to instruct them to sit across from each other in a room so that they were about seven to nine feet apart. The first fourteen subjects were freshman and sophomore women who served as volunteers. They were told not to talk or to communicate in any way. After five minutes, each subject noted on a simple 20-point like-dislike scale how she felt toward the other person. This was repeated for a total of three ratings covering 1 minutes. Each subject was then removed to another room for a short interview. The purpose of the interview was to learn more about what was taking place in the interaction from a subjective point of view. A few days later, the experiment was repeated until a total of five meetings had taken place. During the meeting, two experimenters acted as observers, noting through a one-way screen such things as gesture motions, glances, avoided looks, and other facial or bodily behavior.

We found from our observations and our interviews following each 15-minute meeting that just about every subject experienced considerable

able anxiety and discomfort. This is reminiscent of studies on sensory deprivation, in which S's are placed in settings so that the usual background of auditory, visual, and tactile stimulation is drastically restricted. Our situation, by analogy, might thus be called "social stimulus deprivation."

The Rating Dilemma

In our experiment, the subject actually faces a difficult and unfamiliar problem. Although she has undoubtedly been in nonverbal face-to-face situations with a stranger, the subject could at least keep her feelings to herself. But now she is forced to make up her mind and to reveal her personal reactions. Furthermore, she can see that the other S was rating her, although she cannot see the form or the ratings. Someone is obviously going to see her ratings and she, the subject, will be making herself vulnerable. In addition, S has an obligation to herself, to her own integrity, to express how she really feels.

And yet, on what can she base her reaction? It is inevitable that her rating will reflect, at least in part, her own predilections, her own experience with other people. But in addition she has before her the other unique individual with that individual's ongoing, though muted behavior. At this point, it is postulated that true interpersonal testing takes place and only part of this testing may be done consciously. For example, how does the other subject respond to her and to the small nonverbal cues that she sends out? Is there an attempt at understanding her inquiring glance, or is it coldly ignored? Does the other subject display postural cues of tension, indicating some distress at confronting her? Does the other subject grow increasingly comfortable, indicating some kind of acceptance; or does the other subject treat her as if she were a thing and did not exist? These and many other kinds of readily discernible behavioral exchanges appear to take place. If S is open enough and free enough to take in and to respond to these minor communications and is able to take a quasipublic stand about how she feels, then we may get an authentic record of her reactions to this situation. If she is not free or not sensitive to the present social situation, then we may get either gross projections and distortions or we may get some kind of denial and evasion.

A few *S's* showed such denial and evasion by giving rigidly high favorable ratings. We found that such persons were high scorers on the Berkeley F Scale (authoritarianism).

Changes in Feeling over Time

One of our main questions, then, was what happens to affect ratings over time? The results of interaction in the first three dyads are shown in graphic form.

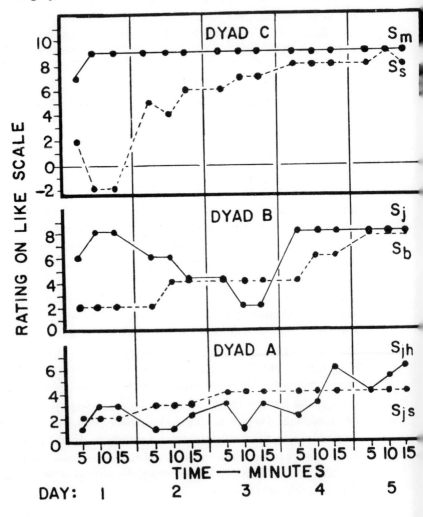

Conflict Between Data Perceived and Data Given by Experimenter

The data suggest that S's tend to converge and to rise in their ratings. In order to determine whether S's could be influenced to lower their like ratings, we arranged three new dyads as before. Then, after S's had an opportunity to experience two sessions, we told each S that the other member of the dyad was rating her lower than she was rating the other member, regardless of the actual ratings. We gave this information during the usual preliminaries before each session. In two of the three dyads, there was an immediate drop in the ratings followed by a slow rise to approximately previous positions. In the third dyad, no change occurred, but this was the only pair where fairly strong dislike ratings had been given independently by each before the feedback session.

In two dyads, we gave positive feedback before their third meeting and their scores either rose or remained at a fairly high level.

A few of the S's suspected that the information given them was spurious, but most apparently accepted it at face value.

Ratings Given Compared to Ratings Expected

Another question we considered was this: Can S's judge the ratings given them by the other person in the dyad? Almost without exception, we found that S's expected ratings that were very close to the ratings they themselves gave the other member (see the graph, page 158). It would seem from this that people anticipate reactions from others commensurate with how they feel toward others; and, frequently, these expectations are way out of line with what the other S actually feels, at least in the ambiguity of the experimental situation. Tagiuri (1958, p. 323) finds the same tendencies.

Anxiety and the Perceived Physical Distance Between Subjects

Because of the ambiguity and stress of the experimental situation, we speculated that when S's are removed from the room in which they confront each other, they will recollect the distance between S's in a distorted way. We found that in six out of seven dyads, the person having the greater manifest anxiety, as measured by the Taylor Scale, judged the distance between S's significantly closer than her partner

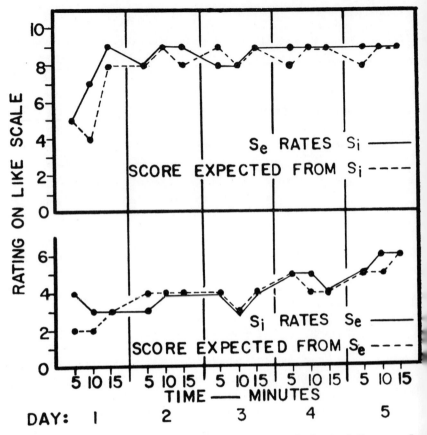

who had less anxiety, and closer than the actual physical distance. In other words, there appears to be a kind of generalized claustrophobic effect for anxious persons in stressful interaction with others.

Self-Regard and Interpersonal Ratings

How do S's regard themselves in relation to how they regard or respond to others? Each of the thirty-six subjects was placed in the dyadic situation as above with a research assistant who acted as the other partner for all subjects. Ratings were made at the end of the first and fifth minutes using the same 20-point like-dislike scale. We divided our group into high and low raters, using five (moderately strong like) as a cutoff point. On the Gough Adjective Check List (Gough, 1961) high scorers on first impression ratings were persons who were more self-accepting than low scorers, with p less than .001. Conversely, low scorers described themselves on the Adjective Check List more critically than high scorers. The difference in self-criticality scores between high and low affect groups was also significant beyond the .001 level. (Gough finds that empirically self-acceptance and self-criticality correlate .15.) The highs and the lows also differed significantly (p less than .01) on the total number of adjectives checked, perhaps indicating a greater degree of expressiveness and less defensiveness on the part of the high scorer. An exception would have to be made of the rigidly high scorer of the affect ratings.

Observation of Dyads

We tried observing dyads through one-way screens in order to relate ratings to the phenomena observed. The meaning of eye contacts appears to be especially important. This is one point at which folklore and literature and clinical observations find some agreement. Simmel (1921, p. 358) has stated, "The union and interaction of individuals is based upon mutual glances. This is perhaps the most direct and purest reciprocity which exists anywhere." Although it was possible to observe gestures and glances, etc., there is a need for increased accuracy and reliability; and perhaps motion picture photography is most appropriate here.

A Concluding Note

These experiments are, as mentioned, frankly exploratory. What is significant is that the procedure lends itself to the study of central and molar phenomena in interpersonal behavior. A number of preliminary findings are supported by other studies, such as those in the symposium on *Person Perception and Interpersonal Behavior* reported by Tagiuri and Petrullo (1958). Goffman's basic ideas in his book, *The Presentation of Self in Everyday Life* (1959), are highly relevant to some of the questions we have raised in this study. Also, personality theorists appear to be shifting away from preoccupation with the person per se, as Blake and Mouton (1959, p. 203) observe in their review of research in personality. "Thus it becomes necessary to develop a way of concept formation which deals with persons and situations simultaneously." In the relatively simple interaction situation here proposed, we may have a way of studying interpersonal behavior in a setting that permits such simultaneous considerations.

To summarize, the impact of strangers on each other in a nonverbal arrangement was measured in terms of changes in like-dislike ratings. Hypotheses concerning the effect of personality variables on the interaction were examined. Fourteen college students in seven dyads met in a series of five 15-minute confrontations. Also, thirty-six S's interacted nonverbally with a standard stimulus subject. The results suggest that attitude toward self is positively related to attitudes toward strangers and that affect ratings expected from others follow closely the rating given to others. High-anxiety S's tended to recall the physical distance between the dyad partners as closer than did the low-anxiety partner, and as closer than the actual distance.

APPENDIX 3

The Language of Movement (with a Note on the Relation between Behavioral Arts and Behavioral Science)*

Talking is such a marvelous thing that once we achieve even a little skill we tend to talk when other kinds of behavior would be more effective. Yet, movement, physical movement of the body, has a language — or is a language in its own right. The language of movement can be

*From "The Language of Movement" by Joseph Luft in *Human Relations Training News*, vol. 9, no. 2, summer, 1965, pp. 4-7, published by the National Training Laboratories. Reprinted by permission.

more precise and more profound than speech. It can of course be more obscure too. Watch a child or watch an adult. It takes years of experience and skill to camouflage bodily language. Still we rarely succeeed completely, and messages get through anyway.

Groups designed to enhance learning about groups and about self can be highly successful in ignoring the language of movement. But it takes a great deal of effort and discipline. The movement will be there. We won't see it, or we will act as if we cannot see it.

Implicit Rules

We have taken over from our culture in general and from traditional teaching-learning arrangements in particular a long list of implicit rules and have applied these rules to groups studying interpersonal and intrapersonal behavior. Here is such a list:

1. We shall sit.
2. We shall face one another.
3. We shall talk.
4. We shall provide time schedules and goals.
5. We shall not touch one another.
6. We shall not yell or yodel or beat on the floor or on the walls.
7. We shall bring people together who can be expected to maintain the implicit rules.
8. We shall have a beginning, a middle, and an end to the arrangements.

The list can be extended. Some of the rules may be useful and necessary; some may not. It is difficult to know ahead of time. The remarkable thing about the history of laboratory groups-on-groups is that some of the implicit rules were not followed, although new ones quickly came in to take their place. The training group is a social invention and like other inventions has continued to evolve and to change. Some day someone will go back and trace these changes, especially the growth and obsolescence of implicit rules.

Movement and Laboratory Training

One of the changes now taking place is the deliberate inclusion of physical movement as part of laboratory procedure. It would seem, on the face of it, that in a laboratory there might be great difficulty in shifting to rules which are unfamiliar. And yet, in my experience this was not the case with participants where body movement was included. (I was fortunate in having the opportunity to work with John and Joyce Weir and George Lehner when I was first introduced to movement as an integral part of a laboratory. I am indebted to Joyce Weir in particular for her sensitive and original contributions in this field.) Under the direction of a person skilled in these techniques it is possible to guide beginners in what seems initially to be a kind of simple dance and child-like play. Background music offers the direct stimulus for tempo, rhythm, and mood, and there is very little serious objection. The main point is to encourage individual expression rather than to emphasize special skills or technique. It is quickly felt and understood that there are no right or wrong ways of moving; nor better nor worse. Most beginners seem to accept this more readily for movement than they do for speech. Though nothing much is said to this effect, the idea is clear, and each is encouraged to lend himself to the mood and to make of it what he can and what he will. A simple movement like walking, hopping, or bouncing to a loosely structured musical theme is left to the individual.

It usually takes but a few short sessions to establish such movement activities as part of the laboratory. Besides satisfying the participants by the sheer pleasure of moving, it soon becomes apparent that everyone wants to talk about it too. Some time is provided in each movement session so that those who wish to may talk or raise questions about the behavior, the feelings, and the interactions that go along with simple movements.

Later, more specific movement activities are taught. By "taught" I mean that the simplest possible structure is provided and the individual is given maximum encouragement for his own improvisation. In fact, the whole movement technique, if technique is the right word, is based on improvisation. (As an aside, one cannot help noting that adults who haven't danced or moved freely for years, may spontaneously begin to express themselves rather eloquently in bodily movement.) In order to give some idea of the procedure I will list some of the activities in abbreviated form and in random order. These activities are preceded by one or more sessions of simple movements or limbering exercises to music.

Illustrative Activities

Mirroring. The group is arranged in pairs, and the instructor asks first one partner to move or to gesture while the other mirrors his movement. The idea is simply that one person tries to do what the other is doing. After a while, the roles are reversed so that the second person has a chance to initiate movements and his partner mirrors everything he does. The next phase is to set the pairs moving with instructions even more free, so that decisions about who leads and who mirrors are left to the participants. In addition, they are told that the leading and following will change but that they will make the shift without verbal communication. Thus, once set in motion, the pairs start as they will and decide for themselves who will lead and how and who will mirror and how frequently changes will take place.

Meeting and parting. This interactional sequence begins with partners, who may be self-selected, moving to opposite sides of the room. With a slowly paced melody to guide them they approach each other with eyes set on partner's eyes; they meet in the middle of the floor, and then move apart. Somehow this one activity seems to tap universal and often emotion-laden experiences of meeting, being together, and parting stored in all of us, and yet it is strongly rooted in the present.

Crossing. Another pattern is to have two columns arranged so that one member from each column moves out to the floor at the same time. Their paths cross as in the letter X. Again it is interesting to observe how each individual moves and how he meets another person, who crosses first and who lets the other pass. Here too, despite its utter simplicity, it is remarkable to see the varieties of ways people interact and to hear later what these interactions evoke. The discussions are filled with all kinds of fresh ways of talking about interaction and with all kinds of new ideas and feelings about the behavior of self and of others.

Group mirroring. A circle is formed and one member begins by clapping his hands in any rhythm he chooses. The others are asked to repeat this pattern one at a time. The idea is for each person to try to put himself in the place of the pattern setter. After going around, each member has a turn at forming a rhythm pattern of his own, to be followed by every other member in sequence. Each thus has a glimpse of what he is doing as portrayed by the others.

Pliable air. Each person is asked to imagine the air about him as consisting of a pliable substance. He might be instructed to shape the soft substance into something like a cocoon or perhaps a cave. Afterward, others may observe how the various participants carry out these instructions, taking note of the style of molding and shaping, the expanse covered, the freedom to use the whole body, to include floor space as well as overhead air space. Other variations can be built on these beginnings by asking persons to work in two's or three's. Again, at the end of an activity participants are free to explore these experiences verbally, if they care to.

Many other kinds of activity can be devised. For example, in the group mirroring, each in turn may be asked to show by gesture and movement such feelings as anger or joy or apprehension. The others, as mentioned, repeat in movement what the model has demonstrated. Another approach is to ask each person to think of a characteristic movement of another member in the group and see whether it is possible for the others to recognize the person through a sample of his movement, a sort of movement leitmotif. Life space is used in another variation. Participants are instructed to enter the life space of another individual, and for the group and the individuals to report on observations and experience. The definition of life space is left to the person.

In a different laboratory, I found that the group had difficulty in describing to a member how his manner of speaking and gesturing affected them. Since there happened to be a large mirror nearby, I asked this participant, who was then engaged in a vigorous interchange with another member, to face the mirror and to continue his debate. Although motion pictures or closed circuit television could serve the same function, the use of a large mirror proved useful in this case. In another instance, I asked a group composed of well-trained and highly articulate members to carry out the simple activity of greeting every other person nonverbally. I set the pattern generally by crossing the floor on hands and knees and bumping into another group member. Since a short time limit was offered, each person was soon on the floor and quickly involved in interacting nonverbally with every other participant. This was immediately followed by a rather intense discussion of the new data and new experience. For one person, this simple kind of interchange with a colleague crystallized the meaning of his whole attitude toward him, a feeling that the person inhibited or controlled him. The other was amazed to learn that he was seen as controlling. And soon they were deeply absorbed in clarifying feelings and impressions.

Rationale

The deliberate introduction of movement activities is intended to serve several purposes.

Communication is facilitated. I believe these procedures can be used to supplement and to broaden interchange of impressions, ideas, feelings, and experiences. It is not a substitute for talk, although at times it seems to go beyond the reaches of verbal communication.

The group atmosphere can be quickly changed. Physical movement seems to create its own atmosphere. When attention shifts from the verbal, the abstract, the ideational, to bodily movement or to simple physical interaction, changes may take place in the psychological climate as well. If music is used, the transformation in group atmosphere may be reinforced and heightened.

The context of discovery may be enlarged. Movement can provide the individual with a wider variety of opportunities to act and to react, to observe self and others when idiosyncrasy is encouraged and accepted. Other work in the laboratory (feedback, verbal testing, reading reports of related studies) emphasizes the gathering of evidence and support for ideas that are stimulated.

Certain conditions for laboratory learning are sharpened. For example, eliminating unnecessary status claims, dealing in the here-and-now, testing one another, encouraging spontaneity, enlarging commitment to the learning process, reducing passivity.

Microstructures are revisited. I believe we are returning to the use of exercises and microstructures in laboratory training. It seems to me that one of the main differences between physical activities such as those described above and the older skill exercises is that the latter were mainly cognitive and external. That is, they dealt with ways of looking at tasks and goals and organizational processes. Body movement calls attention to deep-lying characteristics and to innate processes which influence our interpersonal behavior. There is less reliance on thinking alone. Instead, there is more emphasis on new and direct molar experience. Movement activities can be scheduled within a laboratory design at designated and regular intervals. However, movement may be used at any time, depending on the ability of the staff members and of the participants to improvise. I have a hunch that in the long run the latter approach, in which movement may be introduced at any time depending on need, will have the widest application.

Physical activity can provide a glissando effect. There is value in offering a gradation of experience so that participants need not always go through the initial high tensions of the structureless verbal groups.

Movement can express cultural as well as individual differences. Because movement reaches into present residuals of early experience, cultural qualities that are so important in shaping us may reveal themselves. For persons of the same culture, idiosyncratic differences expressed in the same activity may heighten our awareness of individuality.

Behavioral Arts or Behavioral Science?

One of the nice things about movement as part of laboratory work is that it need not follow certain logical patterns of learning and of change. There appears to be little need to go through prescribed and ordered steps such as observation, induction, analysis, diagnosis, hypothesis formation and testing, synthesis, and so forth. These rational processes do occur, though happily in a less rigid way. A basic reason for this is that we are less apologetic about departing from behavioral science and more fully accepting of an approach which I would call behavioral arts. Both are, of course, important, and though they overlap as to subject matter and perhaps as to long-range goals, they are quite different in the skills, processes, and short-range objectives. One must be careful here in ascribing what to whom. Elegance of equation, for example, as well as other esthetic qualities may be sought by the mathematician or the physicist as well as by the artist.

For the sake of brevity I would say that, as the terms indicate, one approach is more akin to the conventional notion of science, the other is closer to art, but that both at certain times partake of the arts and the sciences.

Another rule of thumb is that the closer we are to dealing with individual persons or groups (on the job, in schools and in the home, in the community), the more we are dealing with artistic matters, with behavioral arts. The more removed from people, i.e., toward data, disparate problems and observations, segmental hypotheses, critical tests of constructs, and general planning, the more safely can we employ the methodology of behavioral science. Each has its own discipline appropriate to its subject matter, each its peculiar strengths and limitations.

By now it must be apparent that other kinds of special activities might find a place in the laboratory, as physical movement appears to be doing. I am aware that at various times laboratories have tried other things such as playreading and acting, singing, prose writing, silence sessions, happenings, dam building, unusual uses of commonplace things (originality trials), community events, and haiku. In a "Laboratory in Personal Growth and Creative Expression," time and materials were provided for painting, including fingerpainting, clay modeling, and verbal-symbolic sessions. The possibilities appear to be limitless. This is not to say that anything goes. Rather, with an understanding of the meaning and purposes of laboratory learning and with an awareness of opportunities and responsibilities involved, there is now a more active challenge to put knowledge and imagination to work.

References

Adelson, Joseph. 1961. The teacher as a model. *The American Scholar* 30:383-406.

Agee, James, and Evans, Walker. 1966. *Many are called.* Boston: Houghton Mifflin.

Argyris, Chris. 1961. Personal versus organizational goals. In *Human relations in administration,* ed. Robert Dubin. 2nd ed. Englewood Cliffs, N.J.: Prentice-Hall.

Asch, S. E. 1956. Studies of independence and conformity: a minority of one against a unanimous majority. *Psychology Monograph,* vol. 70, no. 9.

Barron, Frank. 1964. Diffusion, integration and enduring attention. In *The study of lives,* ed. Robert White. New York: Atherton Press.

Beier, E. G. 1966. *The silent language of psychotherapy.* Chicago: Aldine.

Bennis, W. G. 1964. Patterns and vicissitudes in T-group development. In *T-group theory and laboratory method,* eds. L. P. Bradford, J. R. Gibb, and K. D. Benne. New York: Wiley.

Berne, Eric. 1961. *Transactional analysis in psychotherapy.* New York: Grove Press.

_____. 1966. *Principles of group treatment.* New York: Oxford University Press.

Blake, R., and Moulton, J. S. 1959. Personality. *Annual Review of Psychology* 10:203-232.

Bradford, L. P.; Gibb, J. R.; and Benne, K. D., eds. 1964. *T-group theory and laboratory method.* New York: Wiley.

Brim, Orville G., Jr. 1964. Socialization through the life cycle. Social Science Research Council, *Items* 18:1-5, March. (Published in book form Russell Sage Foundation, 1964.)

Buber, Martin. 1957. Distance and relation. *Psychiatry* 2:97-104.

Buckley, Walter. 1967. *Sociology and modern systems theory.* Englewood Cliffs, N.J.: Prentice-Hall.

Buhler, Charlotte. 1962. *Values in psychotherapy.* New York: Free Press.

Camus, Albert. 1963. *Notebooks.* Vol. 1, 1935-1942. New York: Knopf; London: H. Hamilton.

Cather, Willa. 1936. *Not under forty.* New York: Knopf.

Coan, R. W. 1968. Dimensions of psychological theory. *American Psychologist 23:715-22.*

Colby, Kenneth M. 1964. Psychotherapeutic processes. In *Annual Review of Psychology,* eds. P. R. Farnsworth et al. Palo Alto, California: Annual Reviews.

Cooley, Charles H. 1902. *Human nature and the social order.* New York: Scribners.

Cronbach, L. J. 1958. Proposals leading to the analytic treatment of social perception scores. In *Person perception and interpersonal behavior,* eds. R. Tagiuri and L. Petrullo. Stanford, California: Stanford University Press.

Culbert, S. A. 1967. The interpersonal process of self-disclosure: it takes two to know one. In *New directions in client-centered therapy,* eds. J. T. Hart and T. M. Tomlinson. Boston: Houghton Mifflin.

Cumming, John. 1960. Communication: an approach to chronic schizophrenia. In *Chronic schizophrenia: exploration in theory and treatment,* eds. L. Appleby, J. M. Scher, and John Cumming. Glencoe, Illinois: Free Press.

Dunnette, Marvin D., and Campbell, John C. 1969. Effectiveness of T-group experience in management training and development. *Psychological Bulletin,* vol. 70, no. 2.

Einstein, Albert. 1931. Living philosophies. New York: Simon and Schuster.

Erikson, Erik H. 1951. Midcentury White House conference on children and youth. Health Publications Institute, Inc. (Reprinted in *The adolescent: a book of readings,* ed. J. M. Seidman. New York: Dryden Press, 1953.)

Foote, Nelson N. 1960. Love, in *Marriage and family in the modern world,* ed. Ruth S. Cavan. New York: Thomas Y. Crowell.

Ford, D. H., and Urban, H. B. 1963. *Systems of psychotherapy.* New York: Wiley.

Freud, Sigmund. 1929. *Civilization and its discontents.* Authorized translation by Joan Riviere. New York: J. Cape and H. Smith.

Frost, Robert. 1946. *The poems of Robert Frost.* New York: The Modern Library.

_____. 1949. *Complete poems of Robert Frost.* New York: Holt, Rinehart & Winston.

Gibb, Jack. 1961. Defensive communication. *Journal of Communication* 11:141-48.

Goffman, Erving. 1955. On face-work: an analysis of ritual elements in social interaction. *Psychiatry* 18:213-31.

_____. 1959. *The presentation of self in everyday life.* Garden City, N.Y.: Doubleday.

Good, L. S.; Siegel, S. M.; and Bay, A. P., eds. 1965. *Therapy by design: implications of architecture for human behavior.* Springfield, Illinois: Thomas.

Gough, H. 1961. *Adjective check list.* Palo Alto, California: Consulting Psychology Press.

Halpern, H. M. 1965. An essential ingredient in successful psychotherapy. *Psychotherapy* 2:177-80.

Halverson, Charles F., and Shore, Roy E. 1969. Self-discipline and interpersonal functioning. *Journal of Consulting and Clinical Psychology,* 33:213-17.

Harrison, Roger. 1965. Group composition models for laboratory design. *Journal of Applied Behavioral Science* 1:4.

Haydn, Hiram. 1965. Humanism in 1984. *The American Scholar* 35:12-27.

Jackson, Don D. 1962. Interactional psychotherapy. In *Psychotherapies,* ed. M. I. Stein. Glencoe, Illinois: Free Press.

James, William. 1902. *Varieties of religious experience.* New York: Longmans Green.

Jones, Maxwell. 1968. *Beyond the therapeutic community; social learning and social psychiatry.* New Haven: Yale University Press.

————, and Polak, Paul. 1968. Crisis and confrontation. *British Journal of Psychiatry* 114:169-74.

Journal of Applied Behavioral Science, 1200 17th St. N.W., Washington, D.C. 20036.

Kaplan, Abraham. 1964. *The conduct of inquiry.* San Francisco: Chandler.

Koch, Sigmund. 1961. Psychological science versus the science-humanism antinomy: intimations of a significant science of man. *American Psychologist* 16:629-39.

Laing, R. D. 1961. *The self and others: further studies in sanity and madness.* London: Tavistock.

————; Phillipson, H.; and Lee, A. R. 1966. *Interpersonal perception.* London: Tavistock; New York: Springer.

Lesser, Simon. 1960. *Fiction and the unconscious.* London: Peter Owen.

Lewin, Kurt. 1935. *A dynamic theory of personality.* New York: McGraw-Hill.

————. 1947. Frontiers in group dynamics. *Human Relations* 1:2-38.

————. 1948. *Resolving social conflict.* New York: Harper.

Luft, Joseph. 1953. Interaction and projection. *Journal of Projective Techniques* 17:489-92.

————. 1957. Monetary value and the perception of persons. *Journal of Social Psychology* 46:245-51.

————. 1961. The Johari Window: a graphic model of awareness in interpersonal behavior. National Training Laboratories, *Human Relations Training News* vol. 5, no. 1, pp. 6-7.

————. 1963. *Group processes: an introduction to group dynamics.* Palo Alto, California: National Press.

————. 1964. A way of looking at values. National Training Laboratories, *Human Relations Training News* vol. 8, no. 1, pp. 6-7.

————. 1965. The language of movement (with a note on the relation between behavioral arts and behavioral science). National Training Laboratories, *Human Relations Training News,* vol. 9, no. 2, pp. 4-7.

————. 1966a. On nonverbal interaction. *Journal of Psychology.* 63:261-68.

————. 1966b. Structural intervention. National Training Laboratories, *Human Relations Training News,* vol. 10, no. 2, pp. 1-2.

————, and Ingham, Harry. 1955. The Johari Window, a graphic model of interpersonal awareness. University of California, Los Angeles, Extension Office, *Proceedings of the Western Training Laboratory in Group Development.*

McGrath, Joseph E., and Altman, Irwin. 1966. *Small group research.* New York: Holt, Rinehart & Winston.

Maslow, Abraham H. 1966. *The psychology of science.* New York: Harper and Row.

Miles, Matthew B. 1963. On temporary systems. National Training Laboratories, *Subscription Service,* No. 5.

Mowrer, O. Hobart. 1964. *The new group therapy.* New York: Van Nostrand.

171 **References**

O'Donovan, Denis. 1965. Detachment and trust in psychotherapy. *Psychotherapy,* vol. 2, no. 4, pp. 174-76.

Polanyi, Michael. 1958. *Personal knowledge.* Chicago: University of Chicago Press.

Portmann, Adolf. 1965. The special problem of man in the realm of the living. *Commentary,* November, p. 40.

Reiff, Robert. 1966. The ideological and technological implications of clinical psychology. In *Community psychology,* ed. C. C. Bennett et al. Boston: Boston University.

Rogers, Carl R. 1968. Interpersonal relationships: U.S.A. 2000. *Journal of Applied Behavioral Science* 4:265-80.

Schachtel, Ernest. 1947. On memory and childhood amnesia. *Psychiatry* 10:8-9.

Sears, R. R. 1951. A theoretical framework for personality and social behavior. *American Psychologist* 9:476-83.

Selver, Charlotte. 1957. Sensory awareness and total functioning. *General Semantics Bulletin,* nos. 20 and 21, pp. 5-17.

Simmel, G. 1921. Sociology of the senses: visual interaction. In *Introduction to the science of sociology,* ed. R. E. Park. Chicago: University of Chicago Press.

Simon, Anita, and Agazarian, Yvonne. 1967. *Sequential analysis of verbal interaction (SAVI).* Philadelphia: Research for Better Schools, Inc.

Smith, H. C. 1966. *Sensitivity to people.* New York: McGraw-Hill.

Sophocles. *Oedipus Rex.* Translated by Dudley Fitts and Robert Fitzgerald. New York: Harcourt, Brace & World, 1936, 1960.

Szasz, Thomas. 1961. *The myth of mental illness.* New York: Harper Bros.

Tagiuri, R. 1958. Social preference and its perception. In *Person perception and interpersonal behavior,* eds. R. Tagiuri and L. Petrullo. Stanford, California: Stanford University Press.

———, and Petrullo, L., eds. 1958. *Person perception and interpersonal behavior.* Stanford, California: Stanford University Press.

Tillich, Paul. 1959. The significance of Kurt Goldstein for the philosophy of religion. *Journal of Individual Psychology* 15:20-23.

Towle, Charlotte. 1952. *Common human needs.* New York: American Association of Social Workers.

van Kaam, Adrian L. 1959. Phenomenal analysis: exemplified by a study of the experience of "really feeling understood." *Journal of Individual Psychology,* 15:66-72.

Watson, Robert I. 1967. Psychology: a prescriptive science. *American Psychologist* 22:435-43.

Watzlawick, Paul; Beavin, J.H.; and Jackson, D. D. 1967. *Pragmatics of human communication.* New York: W. W. Norton.

About the Author

Joseph Luft is a professor of psychology at San Francisco State College. He received a Ph.D. degree from the University of California at Los Angeles, with specialization in clinical psychology. He has taught at Stanford and the University of California Medical Center in San Francisco as well as at the University of Florence, where he was senior lecturer on a Fulbright award. He is a diplomate of the American Board of Professional Psychology and a fellow of the American Psychological Association.

In addition to teaching and research, Professor Luft has been interested in experienced-based learning groups, with participants drawn from professional, academic, and community settings.